Curtis,
The best is yet to come

1 Cor. 4:1

REFLECTIONS ON A HIGHER CALL

REFLECTIONS
ON A
HIGHER
CALL

PURSUING EXCELLENCE, INTEGRITY
AND FAITH IN THE MARKETPLACE

DAVID ATCHISON

HIGHER
CALL

AUTHOR'S THANKS

The leadership team of Retail Christian Network—Bob, Chris, David, Jay, Jim and Michael—has so faithfully supported the ministry of RCN. Our early and ongoing conversations inspired the themes that are represented in this book. Special thanks to Jay and Bob, who pushed me to launch our very first breakfast gathering at our annual meeting.

Everyone needs champions who express faith in you. Jim Pye has been that for me. I appreciate your wise counsel and contagious enthusiasm. You model everything "Higher Call" represents. Matthew Ladisa has been another advocate, continually forwarding the *Reflections* to others. Thank you for your example of faithful outreach. Many others repeatedly encouraged me to compile this book—Steve, Jim, John, Sean, Tony, Cindy, Connie and Carol, to name a few. Thanks for the push I needed.

Jay and Kristi Smith at Juicebox Designs not only cared enough to listen to my vision for this project, but skillfully brought it to life through their God-given artistry and devotion to excellence. We also had a lot of fun in the design process. I think it will take many more trips to Chuy's to duly reward your efforts!

Besides being a wonderful writer and editor, John Kramp is the first person who daydreamed with me during college about the possibilities of the marketplace. Your input on this book was golden and so is your loyal companionship. Who knows? "Kratch" may still be on the horizon.

Mark Scott has devotedly walked with me from the pinnacle of my commercial success, through the lowest point of my first company's demise, and every point in between, both professionally and personally. You have never adjusted the intensity of your devotion or affirmation. Our friendship has been such a gift.

Scott Patty is my ministry partner, my prayer warrior, my cherished friend and my pastor. You have helped to shape my theology of God and the workplace over the last twenty years at Grace. Lord willing, we will keep serving together until we are older than dirt.

Besides being my loving wife, my precious "Lainee" has been my long-suffering, masterful editor for over two decades. You have taught me so much about writing and refining my thoughts about each *Reflection* and project we have partnered on all these years. I'm not exaggerating when I say that this book would not have materialized without your assistance.

Trying to name all of you—the list would be too long—reminds me that I am indeed a wealthy man. May God richly bless all of your lives.

CONTENTS

INTRODUCTION

It is no secret that many struggle to make solid connections between their faith and work. The way you face your work week may be very different from the way you approach your day of worship. On the surface, it would seem that spiritual life has little to do with professional life. Often the marketplace demands a callous, concrete mindset that creates tension within our abstract, mystified hearts. Therefore, on Mondays, many inadvertently sever any ties between their job and their faith. This book will challenge this disconnect and unfold many essential, practical and compelling correlations between devotion to God and dedication to work. Most of us fall into one of three categories:

1. **We intentionally separate these two aspects of life.** Work stays at work and faith stays at church (or home). Spirituality has nothing to do with the marketplace and business has nothing to do with religion. What happens at the office stays at the office. What happens on your personal pilgrimage should never interfere in your public enterprises.

2. **We fail at attempts to connect these two facets of life.** Some of us have either tried or observed unsuccessful efforts to integrate faith and work, resulting in awkward or disastrous experiences. Red flags go up when someone introduces themselves as a "Christian" businessperson. Warning bells go off when (any) religion is used as a negotiating chip. All the faith in the world will not make up for unethical or mediocre work. Such displays are not only repulsive to non-believers, but to sensitive followers of Christ as well.

3. **We don't know how to connect our faith and work.** Perhaps you want to link your spiritual convictions with your daily vocation, but you have never known an authentic, insightful, respectful way to do it. The spiritual realm and the marketplace can seem worlds apart. The gap between ancient biblical truths and postmodern cultural realities is challenging—but not impossible—to bridge.

Regardless of where you stand today, God intends for Christians to live out their faith holistically in every arena of life. The Gospel has significant implications for both home and community, for church and the workplace. Navigating through the marketplace for the last thirty-five years has taught me how to apply biblical principles within my workplace, and the impact of displaying biblical conduct beyond the church walls. Your relationship with God should have a very positive influence on your work and on the lives of your colleagues. Genuine faith in Christ should result in outstanding professionalism, exceptional ethics, and a humble demeanor. Those of us who must compete in the marketplace have been summoned by the Creator of work. May we all have spiritual ears to listen, a renewed mind to process, and an obedient will to respond to a higher call.

So he reasoned in the synagogue with the Jews and the devout persons, and in the marketplace every day with those who happened to be there.

ACTS 17:17

A
HIGHER CALL

**EXPANDING YOUR VISION FOR YOUR ROLE
IN THE MARKETPLACE**

I STILL REMEMBER the effect that *Ordering Your Private World* by Gordon MacDonald had on me in 1985. At age twenty-nine, my career in real estate development was moving along at an exhilarating pace. My dreams were clearly in focus. I rejoiced in my beautiful wife and three children in diapers. However, deep within my soul I was wrestling to understand how to balance my burning ambition with my conviction about being on mission for God. MacDonald asked one question that shook my world: "Are we driven people, propelled

by the winds of our times, pressed to conform and compete? Or are we *called* people, the recipients of the gracious beckoning of Christ when He promises to make us into something?"[1]

The issue of being driven or called penetrated the core of my heart. I didn't want to be driven through the streets of the marketplace like a herd of cattle. I didn't want to wake up in my fifties wondering how I ended up someplace I didn't intend to be. I wanted a sense of calling—of hearing God call out my name. I wanted assurance that my life had a purpose beyond the treadmill of achievement and accumulation.

Now I am in my fifties with a little more time to reflect on three decades of experiences in the marketplace and how God's timeless truths address heart issues that are related to faith at work. Let me begin by asking, are you driven or called? *"Faithful is He who calls you, and He also will bring it to pass."* (1 Thessalonians 5:24, NAS)

The sense of divine vision must be restored to man's daily work.

C.S. LEWIS

CONNECTING THE DOTS

PAUL PRAYED OVER the believers in Ephesus that "... *the eyes of your heart may be enlightened so that you will know what is the hope of His calling. . .*" (Ephesians 1:18, NAS) Ephesus (in western Turkey) was a strategic harbor on the Aegean Sea. At the intersection of several major trade routes it was a very active marketplace. As you reflect on his prayer, consider the diversity of the people who inhabited this newly established church. Paul longed for these followers of Christ to awaken to a potent truth—the reality of God's calling for their lives. In the original Greek language *calling* refers to either an *invitation* or *summons*. This communicates the idea of being invited to carry out a particular assignment or mission. Another way to put it is that those called by God are *employed* by Him. God's calling is a personal request to use your talents and skills to carry out His purposes; therefore, each of us should pay closer attention and listen for His voice.

The concept of calling has two distinct facets: the universal and the unique. God's universal calling is for every person to believe, obey, worship, pray, serve and testify of the Gospel in the world. God's unique calling flows from His distinct design and the days He ordained for each individual and the way he or she fulfills God's universal calling. Some religious traditions teach that only pastors, priests, ministers and missionaries are actually called by God. Paul delivered specific instructions to Timothy, who had received God's calling to serve as a pastor (2 Timothy 1:9). However, let's go back to the context of the prayer in Ephesians 1:18. Paul was addressing all the believers in the church, not just the overseers. I find it fascinating that seventy-five percent of the Old and New Testament writers were **not** in vocational ministry. They came from a variety of everyday professions. In addition, Jesus chose twelve disciples from outside the religious order. This is significant for all of us who need help to grasp *"the hope of His calling"* in this generation. Although your profession certainly plays a vital role in God's plans for your life, His calling is larger than any career or occupation.

God does set apart pastors, evangelists, teachers and missionaries; but it is also true that He calls attorneys, consultants, office managers, medical personnel, educators, parents, even politicians—the list is infinite. If you have never made a connection between your work and your faith, listen up! God has intentionally designed your life circumstances to accomplish His purposes. Your God-given skills, talents, passions and experiences are tailor-made for the place you are currently planted. Paul knew how difficult it is to believe that Almighty God would be that involved in your life. That's why he prayed *"that the eyes of your heart would be enlightened."* God wants to connect the dots for you, once you are paying attention.

LORD,

Awaken me to the reality and implications of Your calling on my life. Help me see Your purposes in the ways You have wired me up and guided my path, both personally and professionally. Your plans for my life are so much more strategic and intentional than I ever imagined. Open my eyes so I can see Your hand on my work this week. I really want to make a difference.

UPON REFLECTION

Describe the connections you have made between your career and God's calling for your life.

What does it mean to see with the eyes of your heart? How can spiritual sight be a practical part of your life?

How effectively have you applied your faith to your work over the last year? List some of your biggest questions or concerns.

There is no calling unless there is a caller.

OS GUINNESS

WHOSE CALLING IS IT?

TODAY, A GREAT PRIORITY is being given to "finding your niche" in the marketplace. This helps individuals or companies come to terms with their standing within their particular industry. Finding your role in business is helpful but knowing your purpose in life is essential. Your daily work will never bring the redemptive satisfaction God intends until it fits within the broader context of the calling He has for your life.

Paul's opening prayer for the Ephesians spoke of a glorious inheritance, immeasurable power and growing fullness, but those gifts are not found in ourselves. They are given by God. His grace and mercy toward us compel us to embrace **His** calling for our lives—not **your** calling, **my** calling, even **the** calling will do. You were created for more than a job or a paycheck! God wants to launch you out on assignment for him. Jesus said *"You did not choose me, but I chose you . . ."* (John 15:16) Whether you are planning, marketing, analyzing, managing, designing, negotiating, organizing or anything else, let it register that your current work—enjoyed or loathed—is God's good and wise idea. That may be a revolutionary concept, but to discover then carry out God's calling, you must drop your own agenda and take up His. When you are preoccupied with short-sighted schemes, you will fail to recognize His greater blueprint. As Rick Warren said, "It's not about you. The purpose of your life is far greater than your own personal fulfillment, your peace of mind, or even your happiness."[2]

Over the years, I have known many men and women who have struggled to find their niche in the marketplace. They felt out of place in their job, and assumed they were missing out on something better. For some it was frustration, for others, hopelessness. At times, you may not see the greater purpose or the noble contribution you are actually making. In many cases, you cannot control your circumstances. However, you do have power to choose your mindset and faithfully do the next right thing. God usually doesn't reveal His full plan in one mystical revelation, but He is always faithful to direct your next step. Are you burning the candle at both ends and wondering why you never get ahead? Or are you pursuing excellence one day at a time because you are convinced that it doesn't depend on you alone? Have you found your niche? Faithfully seek God's purposes for your next task, and don't be surprised when your niche finds you.

LORD,

Thank You for reminding me that my career path was not really my idea. You are the One who designed me and assigned me. I would never have dreamed this up myself, but I am beginning to understand that You have called me to something that has implications beyond my own self-interest. I have to be honest, though, and say that I don't fully understand why I am in my current circumstances. That's why I am asking You to grant me a large measure of faith to trust You more. Give me that sense of adventure that You have always intended for me.

UPON REFLECTION

How does your personal agenda line up with what you believe to be
God's agenda for you?

Describe your experience of "finding your niche."
What do you think God is trying to teach you about that?

What is your approach to the mundane aspects of your work?
Do you give them the same energy as the interesting parts?
If not, how will you move in that direction?

Your work is a very sacred matter. God delights in it, and through it, He wants to bestow His blessings on you. This praise of work should be inscribed on all tools, on the forehead and the faces that sweat from toiling.

MARTIN LUTHER

CALLED TO SOMETHING GREATER

THREE BRICKLAYERS WERE asked the same question: *"What are you doing?"* The first one answered gruffly, *"I'm setting bricks."* The next one said, "I'm making a wall." The third one replied enthusiastically, "I'm building a cathedral."[3] Wow. What a difference vision makes in a person's work! Have you ever felt that you were being called to something greater? You may be anxious to move beyond your current job or feel restlessness even in a settled, successful career. Sometimes our yearning or agitation is too deep for words. I'm not sure what God is doing, but I'm confident that you were created for more than a lucrative job or a secure portfolio. Providing for your family is necessary and honorable, but when you follow the whispers within, you may find that God is trying to teach you something new.

"For we are his workmanship, created in Christ Jesus for good works, which God prepared beforehand, that we should walk in them." (Ephesians 2:10) How's that for vision? Are good works limited to spiritual services rendered to a church or charity? God planned that you would do good works like helping a neighbor or praying for a friend, or executing the responsibilities of your job with excellence and serving your company with integrity. Good works go beyond self-interest to the welfare of others. They are not performed to earn God's favor (which is impossible), but to show gratitude to the One who created us and redeemed our lives from eternal disaster.

Matthew's gospel tells you to ". . . *let your light shine before others, so that they may see your good works and give glory to your Father who is in heaven*" (Matthew 5:16). Do you see that your life is not just about you? Does your Light come from yourself? You can evaluate your deeds based on whom they point to—you or God? Whether you are employed by a large company or run your own small business, we all answer to someone greater than a boss or board of directors. Like the bricklayers, your attitude toward work is established by your mindset and your vision. You can choose to look only at the task in front of you (like bricklayer #1), or focus on the short-term (like bricklayer #2), or you can place the task at hand against an eternal backdrop and catch a glimpse at your partnership with God. Like the third bricklayer, set your sights beyond each individual task to your true destiny—seeking the Kingdom of our God who is renewing all things.

LORD,

Open my eyes to new realities. You really have made me for a greater purpose, but I am prone to miss it because my thinking is so small and limited. Even when I feel insignificant or overwhelmed in my job, help me remember that I exist to accomplish what You made me for—Your glory. Don't let me trivialize my tasks this week. Help me to see them as opportunities to serve You and bring pleasure to You. Thank You, Lord, for stirring up my heart and reminding me that You love me more than I imagine. Thank You for giving me a reason to live and love and risk everything to follow You.

UPON REFLECTION

What serves as your greatest motivator to give your best on the job?

How does knowing that you are God's workmanship affect your ability to accurately assess your strengths and weaknesses?

Which parts of your job are difficult to visualize as good works? How will you approach them with a renewed vision today?

*God's own creative activities did not stop at the
beginning of the universe. God is constantly creating
in us, through us, and with us, and to co-create
with God is our human calling.*

MADELEINE L'ENGLE

GOD'S CREATIVITY IN CALLING

HAVE YOU EVER considered how creatively God calls people to Himself? He is the master of the unique and unexpected as He charts the course of your life. Do you believe that God has purposefully arranged your relationships and opportunities for good? Acts 18:1-3 describes Paul's arrival in Corinth after spending time in Athens. Paul was a missionary in Europe and Asia, but do you ever wonder how he managed to travel before trains, electricity, cars or corporate jets? That is where God's ingenuity comes into play. He took a brilliant man and utterly transformed him by Christ's redeeming love, and placed him in the industry of tent-making. This work gave him the mobility and flexibility to travel to foreign markets and connect with friends like Aquila and Priscilla from Italy. They were also tentmakers and followers of Jesus, which opened the door to form a church planting team. Aquila and Priscilla laid the foundation for Paul's work in Ephesus, then moved away to help the church in Corinth. I feel confident that some of the first Corinthian converts came from the tent-making industry. What an interesting way to spread the gospel—through various industries.

God changed a farmer named Gideon into a warrior and military strategist. He ingeniously placed Moses in a Pharaoh's family. He opened the door for a government official named Nehemiah to use his general contracting acumen to rebuild Jerusalem's walls. The majority of Old and New Testament characters were not priests, but God resourcefully linked their unique gifts with their local circumstances to accomplish His ordained purposes. Sometimes unpleasant circumstances open the way for a new calling—Paul met Aquila, not just because they were of the same trade, but because *"Claudius had commanded all the Jews to leave Rome . . ."*(Acts 18:2) You can trust that even the negative events of your life work together for a higher purpose.

That reminds me of my late friend, Ron Gant, who was an executive director of a large trade association. After several years of personal struggle that led to great spiritual renewal, Ron thought about leaving his position to pursue "full time ministry." Then God showed him that by continuing in his industry, he was already influencing people with whom most pastors and ministers could never gain a hearing. With that revelation, Ron gained a whole new vision for his original career path. I hope this makes you wonder what creative plan God has for your workplace and how he may be calling you to take part.

LORD,

*Your Word tells me that all of my days have been
ordained and written in Your book. What a thought!
You have given such care and attention to the details
of my life, more than I will ever realize. I am so
grateful for Your creativity and Your thoughtfulness.
It gives me confidence in the future You have mapped
out for me, and it gives me such great anticipation
of the possibilities that lie ahead. Thank You
for Your presence and companionship in my journey.*

UPON REFLECTION

Why is it important to recognize God's creative callings for the lives of the people around you?

Looking back over your life, can you see how God has orchestrated your circumstances to put you in the position to accomplish His purposes?

How does the awareness of God's creativity encourage you today?

We see time in light of faith in the God of history.
We see how the events of this year are not just a
series of incidents and accidents, happy or unhappy,
but the molding hands of God . . .

HENRY NOUWEN

TIMING IS EVERYTHING

IN BUSINESS, THE old phrase, "timing is everything" really fits. We seek to build all sorts of economic models and sales forecasting tools in order to discern the right time to sell the stock, option the property, raise the capital, expand the chain or increase the staff. When it comes to God's calling for our lives, timing is also crucial. Acts 13:36 confirms this idea: "For David, after he had served the purpose of God in his own generation, fell asleep and was laid among his fathers . . ." God does not work aimlessly. With meticulous calculation He placed David in his given generation and geographical location: 1) part of Christ's lineage; 2) a champion's heart from youth; 3) unabashed love for God when nameless; 4) courageously fighting for God's glory; 5) glorifying God while famous; and 5) repenting before God after dreadful sins. The Bible elaborates further on God's sovereign timing: "And he made from one man every nation of mankind to live on all the face of the earth, having determined allotted periods and the boundaries of their dwelling place." (Acts 17:26)

God placed you in this time period and in your community for a reason—and He didn't miscalculate the schedule. Follow His faithfulness throughout history, generation after generation, and the extraordinary ways His followers changed its course. William Wilberforce is a great example from centuries past. It was no fluke that this young Brit possessed a gift of eloquence which helped him earn a seat in the House of Commons at age twenty-one. It was also no coincidence that God connected him with an array of unique individuals like John Newton, The Clarkson Society and an African named Equiano to champion the abolition of the slave trade long before America considered ending it.

My close friend, Robert "Tiger" Easley, only lived on Earth for forty-seven years. He was involved in real estate, construction and other business interests across Texas, but he was mostly recognized as a man who deeply cared about people, especially the undervalued and underserved. At a young age, he began volunteering countless hours with Big Brothers and Special Olympics. Tiger was an enigma in the "what's in it for me?" generation. Even while he was battling a vicious brain tumor, he modeled a passionate trust in God's timing and provision for his wife and three children.

Will you acknowledge God's flawless timing in your life? Many accuse Him of being too late or not showing up at all. Then they carefully retrace their steps and realize that He was at work, and His timetable had a purpose. Consider Romans 5:6 (TLB): *"When we were utterly helpless with no way of escape, Christ came at just the right time and died for us sinners who had no use for Him."* [emphasis mine] Do not allow impatience to cause you to lose faith that God can use you for something exceptional. Likewise, do not allow grandiose thinking to detain you from carrying out daily responsibilities. As you set your schedule, trust that God's timing is perfect. You may not be asked to slay a literal giant or lead an entire nation, but if you make yourself available to God every moment will become ripe with promise.

LORD,

Sometimes I have a strong sense of Your timing, but other times I am too busy or overwhelmed to notice. Thank You for the great examples of men and women who served your purposes in their generation, especially my friends Ron and Tiger. Renew my mind and heart so I will have the faith and fortitude to serve You right now, right where I am.

UPON REFLECTION

How do you struggle to accept God's timetable for your life? What will help you trust His wisdom about your career?

In what way does the thought of your place in this generation give you a deeper desire to understand God's calling for your life?

Think of a person from world history or the Bible who is an example of God's perfect placement and timing.

REFLECTING ON
MY JOURNEY

In 1987 I completed the best year of my career.
My company increased its portfolio to a value of $85 million. I had earned more money in one year than I ever dreamed possible, and was blessed with loyal employees and wonderful relationships in the business and financial community. We were peaking, and I felt nothing but thankfulness to God. I was married to the love of my life and my best friend. Containing my joy for our three children was impossible. Before I was thirty, I was privileged to serve as a church leader and board member of various non-profits and businesses. My wife jokingly called me the "Golden Boy" because it seemed that everything in my life had been golden. Anyone keeping score would have agreed that I was winning in every area of life. I never saw the storm clouds forming in the background.

Have you ever lined up dominos on a table, thumped the first one, and watched "the domino effect" in successive motion? This is what happened to my business over the next three years. Some of the dominos were the residual effects of the 1986 Tax Reform Act, the implosion of the Savings and Loan industry, the ensuing banking crisis and the collapse of several Texas oil partners. By 1990, I had lost my business, my wealth and my home. It was an excruciating time for my partners, our employees, and my family.

I must note that long before any of those events, I had responded to a compelling call from God to spend more time developing a ministry of discipleship and teaching. I had calculated that it would take about three years to untangle myself from my business ventures and informed my partners of that decision. In the end, my timing was spot on. I just never anticipated the process God would use to make it happen! After some months of transition and healing, I took steps toward launching what is now named Higher Call and was very fulfilled despite my complete financial reversal. Four months later, I was asked to consult about real estate with a national retailer. I agreed to step back into the marketplace, but only as "tent making" work until the ministry took off.

Oh how short sighted I was! Over a period of years, God kept redirecting my focus about work and ministry until I realized that working in the marketplace was the way God was designing my discipleship ministry to professionals. I was not called to be a "professional ministry outsider" but a fellow participant who operates in the same world of market pressures, financial deadlines and business obligations. My work as a retail real estate consultant has opened up amazing doors of ministry in my own industry and beyond. As I reflect on the last twenty-plus years, I am awed by God's creativity and provision. His plans continue to surprise me! It hasn't always been easy and my faith has been stretched way beyond my comfort zone, but I wouldn't trade any of it knowing that God is allowing me to be a part of His plan to redeem the marketplace.

PURSUING
EXCELLENCE
IN THE
MARKETPLACE

RECALIBRATING YOUR DEFINITION OF SUCCESS

REFLECTING YOUR ULTIMATE ROLE MODEL

REDISCOVERING A BIBLICAL WORK ETHIC

BOOKER T. WASHINGTON once said, "Excellence is to do a common thing in an uncommon way." We all appreciate skillfulness. Whether it is a professional athlete, a gifted musician, an innovative entrepreneur or a spell binding speaker we enjoy displays of excellence. God also recognizes quality. Bezalel, Israel's first architect, was handpicked by God to design and construct the first tabernacle and the ark of the covenant. God said, *"I have filled him with the Spirit of God in wisdom, in understanding, in knowledge, and in all kinds of craftsmanship, to make artistic designs for work in gold, in silver, and in bronze."* (Exodus 31:3-4, NAS) God bestows our talents then searches for servants who are willing to apply their skills for His purposes. *"Do you see a man skilled in his work? He will stand before kings; he will not stand before obscure men."* (Proverbs 22:29, NAS) This section will help you recalibrate your definition of success, reflect your ultimate role model and rediscover a biblical work ethic.

Success is that point at which preparation
meets opportunity.

PATRICK MORLEY

BLUEPRINT FOR SUCCESS

I HEARD ABOUT a wealthy businessman who spent his vacation on a fishing trip. One day he happened to notice a fisherman sitting lazily beside his boat. "Why aren't you out there fishing?" he asked. "Oh, I've already caught enough fish for today," replied the fisherman. "Why don't you catch more fish than you need?" posed the traveler. The fisherman thought a minute then said, "What would I do with them?" "Well," came the impatient reply, "You could earn more money . . . then you could buy a better boat so you could go deeper and catch more fish . . . then you could purchase nylon nets, catch even more fish, and make more money . . . soon, you could have an entire fleet of boats and you could be rich like me." The bewildered fisherman asked, "Then what would I do?" "Well, then you could sit back and enjoy life," cried the businessman. "What do you think I'm doing now?" the fisherman exclaimed.[4]

How do you define success? Webster says it is "the degree or measure of attaining a desired end." Another definition is "the attainment of a goal and the enjoyment of the fruits of that achievement." One thing is sure: when it comes to success, you really have to be clear about what you want. Every industry has its icons of accomplishment. Lawyers hope to make partner. Developers aspire to complete a project with national tenants. Sales people shoot to be the top producer. Teachers dream of being Educator of the Year. Our culture identifies *wealth, fame and status* as the highest pinnacles to which one can aspire. Be careful about marshaling all of your time, energy and skill to climb *that* ladder of success. Twenty or thirty years from now, you may wake up to find that the ladder you've been climbing has been leaning against the wrong wall.

Jesus told a parable about a master who entrusted some of his resources to three servants before leaving on a long journey (Matthew 25:14-30). Each servant received a different amount of money, and when he returned, the master checked to see how each handled what had been entrusted to them. One of many truths in this passage is that God does not measure our success by what we have, but by *what we do with what we have*. If you focus on what you wish you had, rather than making the most of your God-given talents, resources or opportunities, you may miss true success. What have you been given? What are you doing with it? You have a skill that you can develop for service. You can be a good steward (or custodian) of the relationships God has placed in your life. You can follow after every prospect that crosses your path. Will you choose to see yourself as God's servant who has been entrusted with both material and human capital to employ until he returns?

LORD,

Thank You for blessing me with spiritual gifts
and practical skills that give me pleasure when I use
them. Thank You for the joy of knowing You and
following Christ. At times the financial resources
You have entrusted me with are more than I need.
At other times they are just what I need even when
it doesn't feel like it. Everything I have comes from
You, so I pray that You will empower me to make
the most of it. I long to one day hear You say,
"Well done, My good and faithful servant."

UPON REFLECTION

How has your definition of success evolved over your career?

What is a healthy balance between the ambition to succeed and contentment with your circumstances?

What corrections or adjustments do you need to make to be sure that you are making the most of all God has given you?

If you are planting for a year, plant grain.
If you are planting for a decade, plant trees.
If you are planting for a century, plant people.

OLD CHINESE PROVERB

SHORT-TERM THINKING

HOW OFTEN HAVE you heard someone share the following strategy and rationale: "I'm not concerned about turning a profit quickly. I just want to focus on doing the right thing and doing things right"? Are you kidding me? In my world, the marketplace demands immediate results. Now think about the opposite approach: "I'm not worried about how this decision will affect us three years from now. Our board expects bottom line results this fiscal year." Sound a little more familiar? Beware! Short-term thinking results in short-term success. How many times has an investment group acquired a company, sold off some of its most lucrative divisions to turn a quick profit . . . only to choke off the long-term potential of the business? Short-term thinking asks questions like, "What are my immediate needs? How can I get quick results? How can I improve my image?" Long-term thinking asks, "What are the most important factors? What can I do now to build for the future? How can I strengthen my character? Where can we improve this company to become a reliable organization for generations to come?"

Jesus told a story about a man whose short-term thinking got the best of him (Luke 12:16-21). He was a wealthy farmer who had been blessed with productive land. On the surface things were going as well as they could, but he began to imagine how he could accumulate even more for himself. In his vain imagination, he convinced himself that he controlled his own destiny, and built larger barns in which to store more crops. That would really secure his future. Suddenly God made the farmer's short-term thinking even shorter. *". . . God said to him, 'Fool! This night your soul is required of you, and the things you have prepared, whose will they be? So is the one who lays up treasure for himself and is not rich toward God."* (Luke 16:20-21)

While our culture continues to be obsessed with finding short cuts to success, you must develop the wisdom to take a longer view of life. Are you a short-term or long-term thinker? Do you focus more on your schedule than your soul? Are you spending all of your prime time and resources building up your bank accounts, or investing in eternal things that will reap perpetual assets? To become rich toward God you must learn to think long-term by projecting beyond this life, and by envisioning things that will truly last.

LORD,

Why do I get so easily caught up in the things that I can see and touch, even when I know they won't last? Give me a longer view of life. Help me see the eternal backdrop in everything I do this week. Remind me that only what I complete for Your glory has unending value. Teach me to value Heaven's treasures more than Earth's—and the amazing gift of new Life with You.

UPON REFLECTION

What dynamics are driving your profession toward short-term rather than long-term thinking?

How can you develop a longer view of life? Try to make a list of the things you are pursuing that will last forever.

Name some long-term implications of short-term thinking? How have you fallen into this trap?

[Jesus] didn't come to give us formulas.
He came to give us a new mindset—
one that has a turnaround mentality.
In fact, the word repent *means to turn around.*

LAURIE BETH JONES, *JESUS, CEO*

A TIMELY TURNAROUND

CAN YOU IMAGINE Alfred Nobel's shock when he read his own obituary in the morning newspaper? *"Alfred Nobel, the inventor of dynamite, who died yesterday, devised a way far more people could be killed in a war than ever before, and he died a very rich man."* It was actually the Swedish chemist's older brother who died; the newspaper reporter had written the wrong epitaph! That experience had a profound impact on Nobel. He wanted to be known for something other than an invention that destroys people, so he initiated the Nobel Prize, an award for scientists and writers who foster peace. Nobel declared that "Every man ought to have a chance to correct his epitaph in midstream and write a new one."[5]

Sometimes it takes an appalling event to see ourselves more clearly and do a 180°. Alfred Nobel had already accomplished a great deal, and had amassed great wealth, but recognized that his life was really a failure. Thankfully, he still had time to make a dramatic change. Have you ever thought you were operating with "eyes wide open" only to realize that you were blinded to spiritual realities? The Apostle Paul was another person whose direction radically changed. He claimed, that *". . . whenever a person turns to the Lord, the veil is taken away."* (2 Corinthians 3:16, NAS) If you will turn away from the g-o-d you have created in your own mind and set your sights on the Living God revealed in the Bible, you will begin to view your life more accurately. Then God will shed more light on the direction He is leading you.

Will you pay closer attention to every area of your life, including the way you have been working? Will you ask God to help you turn away from futile endeavors before it is too late? According to Taylor and Wacker's futurist book, *The 500 Year Delta*, the most asked question of our day is: "If I'm doing so well, why do I feel so bad?"[6] Don't turn toward the piles of work on your desk until you spend some time contemplating how your epitaph would read today. Thankfully, it is not too late to change directions.

HEAVENLY FATHER,

I am stopping right now to reflect on Your presence
in this place. You are overseeing everything I've been
aiming for. Now I need to consult with You before
I take another step or make any other plans for my
week. Do I need to turn around and go in a different
direction? I know I need Your light to stay on the
path You have chosen for my life. Thank You for
the gift of Your wisdom about what significance
means in terms of Your kingdom purposes.

UPON REFLECTION

What do you think your epitaph would say if your associates, clients and co-workers had to write it today?

How satisfied are you with the current trajectory of your life? Following that course today, where are you headed?

What changes would you like to make in your life or your career but wonder if it is possible?

*If a man is called to be a street sweeper, he should sweep
the streets even as Michelangelo painted, or Beethoven
composed music, or Shakespeare composed poetry.
He should sweep streets so well that all the hosts of
heaven and earth will pause to say, "Here lived a great
street sweeper, who did his job well."*

DR. MARTIN LUTHER KING

FLOURISHING WHEREVER YOU ARE

HAVE YOU EVER awakened to find yourself in a situation you never
thought you'd be? Maybe you planned to work in a different profession,
or expected your financial status to be more secure. It's possible that absolutely nothing about your life today is going according to your plans. If so,
multiply your situation by one hundred and that might equal Joseph's circumstances (Genesis 37). That confident young man, whose bright future
was revealed in a dream, experienced an impossible level of sibling rivalry.
Ten jealous half-brothers plotted to take his life . . . but decided instead to
sell him into slavery. Joseph was carted off to Egypt, where he was promptly
sold again. Try to imagine what he thought about God's plans at that point.

Joseph's God-sized vision must have seemed like a terrible mistake.
Anyone of us might despair over the death of a plan we thought God re-
vealed to us. However, in a foreign land, estranged from his family, where
freedom—much less reigning—was unattainable, Joseph's true character
shone forth. *"When Joseph was taken to Egypt by the Ishmaelite traders, he was purchased by
Potiphar, an Egyptian officer. Potiphar was captain of the guard for Pharaoh, the king of Egypt.
The LORD was with Joseph, so he succeeded in everything he did as he served in the home of his
Egyptian master. Potiphar noticed this and realized that the LORD was with Joseph, giving
him success in everything he did. This pleased Potiphar, so he soon made Joseph his personal*

attendant. *He put him in charge of his entire household and everything he owned. From the day Joseph was put in charge of his master's household and property, the LORD began to bless Potiphar's household for Joseph's sake. All his household affairs ran smoothly, and his crops and livestock flourished.*" (Genesis 39:1-5, NLT) [emphasis mine]

Don't miss the significance of what God was doing behind the scenes, and how Joseph was responding to it. Rather than lying down to die or growing bitter toward God, wherever he was placed Joseph continued to thrive. He proved himself both diligent and loyal as he advanced from slave, to servant, to overseer (Potiphar's Chief Operating Officer). We do not know how long these promotions took, but mastering his work and earning Potiphar's trust didn't happen overnight. Joseph had no input in where he worked, yet he labored with his whole heart. As he worked faithfully and matured inwardly, God plainly displayed Joseph's distinctive leadership qualities. Astonishingly though, even more adversity awaited him. Joseph was unjustly thrown into prison then forgotten for two years . . . but not by God or the chief jailer who also found him to be helpful and trustworthy.

Make time to read the whole story, for ultimately, Joseph became the most powerful man of his time. Look over your own work history and evaluate whether you have always given your best, even in less than ideal situations. That can be a challenge for a generation that has been so preoccupied with getting to the next phase that we despise or devalue our current circumstances. You can learn workplace wisdom from all that Joseph modeled and the truth that "The Lord was with Joseph." News flash! The Lord is present within every believer in Jesus. Despite anyone who overlooks you or sells you out, God will accompany you as you walk in this world (Matthew 28:20). If you have not crossed the line of entrusting your entire life to Jesus Christ, you have the opportunity to claim the same promises Joseph held onto during his surprising course of disappointment and deliverance. While you cannot always control your circumstances, you can choose to rely on God's wise direction and guidance. That confidence freed Joseph to devotedly carry on wherever he was. Imagine what could happen if all of Jesus' followers, scattered throughout the marketplace, trusted God in this way today.

LORD,

You know I want to please You with my efforts, but I know my heart and the things that hold me back. I spend too much time and energy thinking about how to manage things that You never intended me to control. I have often been distracted by discontentment, restlessly wishing for the "next thing" instead of accepting that You have things to teach me where I am right now. Help me to lean into Your sovereign view of the future, so I am free to flourish wherever You put me, now.

UPON REFLECTION

Where are you on your career path and how is that different than where you expected to be at this point in your life?

What is your track record concerning your response when you've been in less than ideal professional circumstances?

When you read "*the Lord was with Joseph,*" how does that make you feel about your own journey so far?

Christians can be so heavenly minded that they are no earthly good, or they can be so earthly minded that they are no heavenly good.

UNKNOWN

DISCERNING THE ENDGAME

I AM A FAN of good spy movies because I love the suspense and intrigue of an unpredictable plot. In this movie genre, if you want to know whether a character is trustworthy, you have to know their *endgame*. In an odd sort of way, the marketplace is similar to a spy movie. When you are working with a client or competitor it is essential to know their ultimate goals and yours—the endgame.

The people of Babel had an endgame when they began building their big tower to paradise. "*. . . Come, let us build ourselves a city and a tower with its top in the heavens, and let us make a name for ourselves . . .*" Genesis 11:4 captures the essence of what lies behind most schemes to make it to the top. When we are honest, isn't our underlying motive about the same? "Come, let us craft for ourselves a lavish lifestyle; and let us construct for ourselves an illustrious image."

Thousands of years ago, Augustine described human history using the metaphor of two cities diametrically opposed to one another: the City of Man and the City of God. The City of Man seeks to elevate and applaud itself; whereas, the City of God seeks to glorify and exalt God.[7] Here lies the tension you and I encounter every day. Followers of Jesus Christ are "citizens" of the City of God, but also "sojourners and foreigners" who must work and live in the City of Man. (see Ephesians 2:19 and 1 Peter 2:11)

How will you live with this friction? Retreating is not the answer; nor is denying that a conflict exists. Conceding to a "City of Man" agenda is definitely not the solution. Instead, we find a straightforward answer in

Hebrews 11:9-10 (NAS), "*By faith [Abraham] lived as an alien in the land of promise, as in a foreign land, dwelling in tents, with Isaac and Jacob, fellow heirs of the same promise; for he was looking for the city which has foundations, whose architect and builder is God.*" God will one day summon us to inhabit a perfectly designed realm that far exceeds anything we can imagine now. For the time being we are residents of Earth who are dedicated to living, working and loving according to the higher call of our heavenly citizenship. Where does your citizenship lie today? Are your eyes fixed on the City to come or what you can build for yourself? What is your endgame?

LORD,

I am aware that my real habitat is not the marketplace I function within as a temporary resident. My real home is Heaven with You. On the other hand, You have placed me here for Your glory and the welfare of my city. Keep me from both self-pity and false superiority. Instead give me Christ's compassion and respect for those around me. Give me courage and vision to serve others with greater integrity and a God-sized endgame.

UPON REFLECTION

Where are the conflicts between the values of your faith and the values of the world's system?

How aware have you been of the spiritual needs of those around you at work?

When do you take time to consider God's higher purposes for your workplace?

The man without a purpose is like a ship without
a rudder—a waif, a nothing, a no man.

THOMAS CARLYLE

GOD WORKS WITH PURPOSE

SINCE GOD MADE US in His likeness, we should look to Him as the perfect example for all things—including our work. Nature gives evidence that God is a purposeful worker. Our growing understanding of the land, sky and sea reinforces that His labor is neither random nor ordinary. In all the realms of God's cosmos, everything has a meaningful function and God is knowledgeable of its purpose.

The Lord designed the sun to govern the day and the moon to govern the night (Genesis 1:14-16). He created the fascinating cycles of water—rising up to make clouds, traveling along in the atmosphere then falling as rain, which runs into streams and rivers and oceans. Water is only one critical facet that sustains life for all living things. With the same determination, God created humans with intricate workings and the ability to be purposeful and productive like He is. Ephesians 2:10 says, *"For we are His workmanship, created in Christ Jesus for good works, which God prepared beforehand, that we should walk in them."*

Have you stopped to consider that God is still a purposeful worker? He continues to labor over His greatest masterpiece, the human race. He indescribably and omnisciently directs the universe, yet is well acquainted with every living soul. We cannot fathom His vast thoughts or ways, except to trust that they are not aimless or arbitrary. *"And we know that for those who love God all things work together for good, for those who are called according to his purpose. For those whom he foreknew he also predestined to be conformed to the image of his Son, in order that he might be the firstborn among many brothers. And those whom he predestined he also called, and those whom he called he also justified, and those whom he justified, he also glorified."* (Romans 8:28-30) This is not illogical or impulsive effort.

Because God is a purposeful worker, you can learn to be more intentional in your own vocation. This does not mean that everything you are required to do will make sense to you or have an obvious rationale. We live in a fallen world and work within broken systems, so pointless tasks and irrational goals are likely to challenge and burden each of us. Here are two ways you can become more purposeful in your work.

1. **Evaluate all of your functions and operations to define their purposes.** Why do you return phone calls, compose e-mails, develop schedules, communicate with vendors, calculate returns, study market trends, service clients' needs, fill out progress reports, etc.? Take time to think through the ultimate purposes for each task—even the annoying, seemingly insignificant jobs should lead to a useful outcome. Those tedious reports could help the decision makers set the direction of your company. The numbers you crunch may allow your neighbors to receive better health care. Your carefully worded, hand-written correspondence may provide encouragement and appreciation your vendors receive from no one else.

2. **Allow intentionality to drive your priorities.** We are often the victims rather than the masters of our schedules. We allow the urgent rather than the important to eat up our time and energy. What are the three most important things you need to accomplish this week? If you want a shot at getting them done you must adjust your schedule to protect the most strategic ones. Just as God designed our world to function in an orderly fashion, He will help you arrange your personal and public undertakings to accomplish what He intends.

LORD,

You are my example, my highest ideal. Everything You do has a higher purpose, even if I can't grasp it. I confess that I approach many responsibilities with a chaotic style. Help me to live according to Your pattern, and work with Your intentionality and orderliness even in the smallest task I am given.

UPON REFLECTION

Have you ever considered God as a role model for your work? How does this perspective affect the way you approach your responsibilities in the workplace?

What tasks in your occupation have the greatest sense of purpose? Which seem to have the least significance?

As you survey your contributions at work, list some specific ways you should reprioritize so you can work more effectively.

Everyone thinks of changing the world. But no one thinks of changing himself.

LEO TOLSTOY

GOD PLANS HIS WORK

EVERYTHING IN GOD'S immense creation required meticulous planning and precision. The Solar System and all of the visible stars are in different orbits around the core of the Milky Way galaxy. A star's apparent brightness changes as it moves toward or away from us. Sirius is currently the brightest star in the Earth's night sky, but it has not always been so. Canopus has persistently been the brightest star over the ages. Scientists have projected which stars will be brightest over the next five millions years, but none can envision God's plan for mankind, for the universe, or for Heaven.

The Bible reveals some of God's intricate plans for the Hebrew people and their original transportable tabernacle (Exodus 25–40). Its unique blueprint should impress any architect. Generations later, a fixed temple was constructed, destroyed, rebuilt then demolished again. Unlike human structures, God's plans cannot fail or be thwarted: "*The LORD brings the counsel of the nations to nothing; he frustrates the plans of the peoples. The counsel of the LORD stands forever, the plans of his heart to all generations. Blessed is the nation whose God is the LORD, the people whom he has chosen as his heritage!*" (Psalm 33:10-12)

Observing how God has worked among His people gives us a pattern for our work in the marketplace. Planning is one criterion that deserves higher value. How are your planning skills? Are you prone to over- or under-plan? Jeremiah 29:11-13 reiterates how faith in God's plan factors into this process: "*'For I know the plans I have for you,' declares the Lord, 'plans for welfare and not for evil, to give you a future and a hope. Then you will call upon me and come and pray to me, and I will hear you. You will seek me and find me when you seek me with all your heart.'*" Here are two important principles to plan your work in a fruitful, faithful manner.

1. **Embrace the reality that planning is a vital part of working well.** Don't separate the functions of planning and execution ("I must hurry to finish this planning so I can get some work done"). Planning is indispensable work. The old saying, "Plan your work and work your plan" is still sound advice. At the beginning of the year, the month, the week, the day, discipline yourself to schedule time for strategic planning. From fifteen minutes to a whole morning, planning time will help you avoid pitfalls and achieve goals. Read Luke 14:28-30 about the foolish builder who launched a project without carefully calculating the expenses. Wise planning honors God and increases your productivity.

2. **Understand the relationship between planning your work and working by faith.** There is a difference between faith and presumption. Take care not to impulsively make plans then presume that God will deliver them. Developing an audacious business plan does not guarantee its success (James 4:13-16). Acknowledge your partnership with God as you plan. *"The mind of man plans his way, but the Lord directs his steps."* (Proverbs 16:9, NAS) When you carefully plan a joint venture with God, He will guide you toward the best and most honorable strategy.

CREATOR GOD,

You have called me to bring all of my knowledge and skill to the table, and dedicate my plans to You. More often than not, I lack the discipline to plan according to Your pattern. Recognizing how You plan Your work inspires me to adopt a new daily work style. Thank You for giving me the mind of Christ to provide special assistance as I plan. Thank You for the promise in Proverbs 16:3— "Commit your works to the Lord and your plans will be established." I place them in Your hands right now.

UPON REFLECTION

Estimate the time you spend on the *work* of planning each day. Evaluate your effectiveness in planning over the last year. What changes can you make for this quarter?

Which are you more prone to: presumptive faith (wishful thinking) or cynical faith (negative thinking)? How can you develop a healthier balance of working by genuine faith (God-directed thinking)?

How will the truth of Proverbs 16:9 change the way you plan your next project?

We ought not to look back unless it is to derive
useful lessons from past errors, and for the purpose
of profiting by dearly bought experience.

GEORGE WASHINGTON

GOD EVALUATES HIS WORK

IN THE FAST pace of today's marketplace, reflection and appraisal are undervalued. If we hope to keep up with our industry's ever-changing dynamics, there is little time to retrace our steps. On the contrary, when you seek to emulate a work style shaped by God's attributes, you will note that **God appraises His work**. By whatever means God created our universe, a very complex project to say the least, the Scriptures tell us that after each day *"God saw that it was good."* He took time to observe, assess and celebrate His accomplishments. Even though God is perfect in all His ways, He modeled self-appraisal for our benefit. Our all-knowing Creator already grasped the big picture, but once completed, He carefully "looked over" all the details and their broader impact (Genesis 1:1-31).

The Greek philosopher Socrates said "The unexamined life is not worth living." Jeremiah recorded God's instructions for such an inspection: *"Let us examine and probe our ways, and let us return to the Lord."* (Lamentations 3:40, NAS) The principle of evaluation applies to our work and every area of our lives. We must deliberately set aside time, then orient ourselves to consider God's appraisal of our effort, our effectiveness and where we have abandoned His path. Here are some helpful questions to reflect on each week.

What did I learn? What did I accomplish? What was the quality of my work? What opportunities did I seize? What did I miss? What was my greatest challenge, and how did I handle it?

Whom did I serve? Whom did I influence? Whom did I neglect or hurt in any way? In what ways did my work bring glory to God instead of myself?

How can I manage my time better next week? How do my current projects relate to a bigger vision or calling? How did this week expose my true character? How will I turn away from the ineffective, the inappropriate or the immoral? How will I return to God's principles for efficient, ethical and honorable conduct?

I pray that these evaluation tools will help you strive to stay more focused and accountable as you move forward—not to perfection—but to greater excellence at work for God's glory.

LORD,

I have not consistently slowed down long enough to
have the true picture of how I am living and working.
I know this pleases the Enemy, and my real desire is
to please You. Give me the courage and discipline
to evaluate my days, my work and my relationships.
I know there are areas where I have drifted away
from Your principles and need to return to a more
Christ-honoring behavior and work ethic.

UPON REFLECTION

How much time do you set aside each week to look back and evaluate your work? What impact could this have (positive and negative)?

When was the last time you looked back on a job and *"saw that it was good"*?
How would you rate your current level of satisfaction and fulfillment at work?

What practical measures can you employ to make evaluation time a valuable part of your weekly routine?

*I have fought the good fight. I have finished
the race. I have kept the faith.*

THE APOSTLE PAUL

GOD FINISHES WHAT HE STARTS

THINK OF HOW the Yale student felt when he received a "C" on a paper that proposed a reliable overnight service to deliver letters and packages. If Fred Smith had not finished what he started, we wouldn't have Federal Express. Masuru Ibuka, once asked, "Why can't we remove the recording function and speaker and put headphones with the player?" People thought he had lost his mind, yet Ibuka persisted and gave us the Sony Walkman. Then came Steve Jobs and that Apple idea . . . you get the picture. One of the most encouraging verses in the Bible is found in Philippians 1:3-6: *"I thank my God in all my remembrance of you, always in every prayer of mine for you all making my prayer with joy, because of your partnership in the gospel from the first day until now. And I am sure of this, that he who began a good work in you will bring it to completion at the day of Jesus Christ."* Despite our spiritual ups and downs, God never gives up on us or stops working in us. What a wonderful promise. He will perfect the good work He started.

A golden thread runs throughout biblical history—first in creation, then in every generation traced by the Old and New Testaments. God is moving both creation and humanity toward its full redemption [deliverance, recovery, liberation]. Noah worked for *one hundred twenty years* to build an ark per God's design, and God finally carried out judgment and mercy on the corrupted Earth. The Lord allowed the Israelites to suffer four hundred years of slavery under the Egyptians, yet none of the ten plagues preceding their release harmed the Israelites. After forty more years of wavering and rebellion, God faithfully accomplished their liberation and resettlement in their promised homeland. Centuries before it came to pass, God foretold through many prophets the precise details of His plan to redeem mankind from the curse of sin and death at just the right time in history. We possess the written record that clearly explains His plan to come to us in human form and finally defeat these foes. That plan included death on a cross, then rising to life again. What were Jesus' last words on the cross? "It is finished!" Two millennia later, God is able and committed to completing His plans for every people group and person who will receive Him. We can trust that God will triumph, and good will prevail.

Finishing what is started is a critical workplace lesson. The trend is to work only when required and to quit when things get rough—in our jobs, our relationships and even our churches. Instead, Christians are called to steadfastly persist until fully completing the smallest chore or the most comprehensive project. Finishing is not to be confused with success or failure—some setbacks are inevitable in business. Ultimate success incorporates the code of finishing what you start, even when there are obstacles along the way.

At the 1968 Olympics, John Stephen Akhwari represented Tanzania in the marathon event. During the race he stumbled and fell, severely injuring his knee and ankle. By 7:00 p.m., an Ethiopian won the race and the other competitors had finished. Only a few thousand spectators were left when a siren caught their attention. Through the gate limped Akhwari with his leg wrapped in a bloody bandage. People cheered the courageous man as he completed the final lap of the race. A reporter asked the question on everyone's mind: "Why did you continue after you were so badly injured?" He replied simply, "My country did not send me 7,000 miles to begin a race; they sent me to finish the race."[8] What is on your desk today that needs to be completed? On what assignment have you lost steam? Your current project is a small part of God's bigger "race." By the strength of His example and the power of His Spirit you can see them through, one step at a time.

> **LORD,**
>
> *I am reminded that I easily drop ideas or put projects*
> *on the back burner if I don't find instant success.*
> *Teach me to recognize what should be finished no*
> *matter how difficult it feels or how long it takes,*
> *and which idea's time simply hasn't come. I want*
> *to be faithful to finish the assignments You have*
> *given me today.*

UPON REFLECTION

Are you more effective initiating new projects or finishing them? What contributes to that tendency?

Describe the feeling you had the last time you persevered and finished a long and difficult assignment. Compare that to your emotions related to an endeavor you started but never finished.

What role does the fear of failure play when it comes to abandoning things you start?

Being hurried comes naturally, while being at rest
requires an ongoing appraisal of priorities.

TIM KIMMEL

GOD PRIORITIZES REST

IN THE DEEP jungles of Africa, a traveler set out on a long trip. He had high hopes for a speedy journey and the natives he hired to carry his heavy cargo walked quickly and traveled far on the first day. The second morning the tribesmen refused to move. They just sat, as though deep in thought. When asked about this strange behavior, they said that they had gone too fast the first day, and they were waiting for their souls to catch up with their bodies.[9]

How is your pace these days? After creating the world, God (who does not get tired) modeled rest for us. "By the seventh day God completed His work which He had done, and He rested on the seventh day from all His work which He had done." (Genesis 2:2, NAS) He also gave clear instructions about how humans should follow suit: "You shall work six days, but on the seventh day you shall rest; even during the plowing time and harvest you shall rest." (Exodus 34:21, NAS) Notice that we are told to rest even during our busiest seasons. You are used to considering your work ethic, but what about your rest ethic?

Every industry has peak times. Farmers probably understand that the best. For an accountant, it's tax season. For a meteorologist, it's hurricane season. For a cook, it's the lunch hour. Even when you're maxed out you are instructed to make time for rest. If the God of the universe prioritized rest, shouldn't we? Instead, we continue to devise new ways to squeeze more into our week. We have countless gadgets that promise to save time, yet most of us leave ourselves no margin. Thomas Kelly described the unguided life as an "intolerable scramble of panting feverishness."

Take some time to weigh in on these things:

1. **Consider your attitude about rest.** Your answer reflects the state of your faith. Your ability to stop reflects your belief about God's ability to run the universe without your assistance. It is not noble to work more hours or days. It may be arrogant and faithless! Psalm 127:2 (NAS) warns: "*It is vain for you to rise up early, and to retire late, to eat the bread of painful labors: for He gives to His beloved, even in his sleep.*" Do you believe that God can provide for your family if you intentionally choose not to "burn the candle at both ends"? What if you draw a boundary with your employer about working unpaid extended hours? That's a hard one!

2. **Consider how to rest in a restorative way.** Read a book or take a walk with your child. Enjoy coffee and quiet conversation with your spouse. Fish or play golf with a friend. Listen to good music while you exercise. Take a nap or watch a movie between projects. Dine outside or "potluck" with neighbors. Again, planning ahead for time-outs, recreation and retreats is not just good for your body but for your soul. The most important principle is that rest is customary and continual. The commitment to rest involves certainty that "*. . . in Him all things hold together.*" (Colossians 1:17) It also involves sharing the load with Jesus, who offers His full support: "*Come to me, all who labor and are heavy laden, and I will give you rest. Take my yoke upon you and learn from me, for I am gentle and lowly in heart, and you will find rest for your souls. For my yoke is easy, and my burden is light.*" (Matthew 11:28-30)

JESUS,

You know that consistently taking time off and getting enough rest at night—especially during crunch times—is a real weakness for me. I pretend I am exempt from Your clear model for replenishing physical, mental, emotional and spiritual strength. You have revealed that my attitude comes from a lack of faith in Your method of living. Train me to build moments, hours and days of restoration into my calendar instead of claiming I don't have time. Remind me that not everything in the universe revolves around me or depends on me—thank You for that! Amen.

UPON REFLECTION

What is your track record when it comes to rest?
How is this impacting you physically, spiritually, emotionally and mentally?

How have you observed that rest actually increases productivity?

What changes do you need to make so you can be replenished (or restored) to holistically balanced health?

Labor was not punishment; neither was it an
afterthought. Labor was the design. It was God's
way of filling man's days with pleasant,
meaningful activity.

BILL HYBELS

LEANING INTO THE PLEASURE OF WORK

SEVERAL YEARS AGO, I was on a site tour with my broker and friend, Chris Palmer. We had been on the road the entire day before, looking for potential store sites, and the next day we had worked late into the night. I have to admit, by the third morning I was dragging. When I got in the car, Chris was waiting with a fresh cup of Starbucks coffee. He smiled and said, "I love my job." He wasn't just trying to get me motivated for another long day—he really meant it. Chris is a professional in every sense of the word. He knows his stuff, does his homework and loves his work.

Do you love your job or do you have trouble finding a good reason to get out of bed in the morning? Every type of work has difficult or unpleasant aspects, but on the whole, work was meant to be enjoyed. Ecclesiastes 5:18-19 has a way of putting this in perspective: "Behold, what I have seen to be good and fitting is to eat and drink and find enjoyment in all the toil with which one toils under the sun the few days of his life that God has given him, for this is his lot. Everyone also to whom God has given wealth and possessions and power to enjoy them, and to accept his lot and rejoice in his toil—this is the gift of God."

Let that sink in for a minute. Our work is a reward, a gift given straight from the hand of God. Notice that it references the work itself, not the income derived from it. Not the benefits or stock options or prestige. We have been designed to enjoy the exertion of our energy toward productive activity. Real pleasure is found when we put our God-given skills and talents to work. Don't worry, I live in the same marketplace you do. I know this kind of thinking goes against the grain. It has been drilled into all of us to get ahead and find jobs that will enable us to make lots of money and earn the most accolades.

There is nothing wrong with carving out a great career path or making money; however, some of us are running so fast to chase down the booty the marketplace promises, that we miss out on the simple pleasure of doing our daily work. Even if no one in your office or industry notices your efforts or contributions, God does. After all, who are you really working for? Think about the tasks you engage in this week. Whether it's making sales calls, solving technical problems, working on personnel solutions, scheduling out a project or crunching numbers, get a cup of coffee or your favorite beverage, smile and thank God for (or ask God for) genuine pleasure in your work.

LORD,

Thank You for giving me work to do today.

When I complete a task it is satisfying to know that

You are the one who enabled me to do it well. It is so

rewarding to use the aptitudes You have given me.

I confess that too often I waste time worrying about

things I can't control, and miss out on the daily

delight You provide through colleagues like Chris.

Help me concentrate on my job today, while trusting

You to do Yours.

UPON REFLECTION

Who or what is robbing you of the joy and pleasure God intends for your work?

What do you love most about your job?
What do you hate about it?

What makes it difficult for you to believe that work is a reward? How can you change your view of the things you dislike about your job?

The great word of Jesus to His disciples is "abandon."
When God has brought us into the relationship of
disciples, we have to venture on His word; trust
entirely to Him and watch that when He brings us
to the venture, we take it.

OSWALD CHAMBERS

PUTTING YOUR HANDS TO THE GOOD WORK

ONE OF MARK Twain's boyhood friends who was jealous of the writer's fame, said, "I know just as many stories as Mark Twain. All he did was write them down."[10] This is a classic example of how the marketplace is divided into Doers and Dreamers. Dreamers are happy to point out that there is nothing distinctive about their colleagues who are highly praised. Few Dreamers are busy making the most of their opportunities, while the Doers simply apply themselves with diligence and excellence to the good work within their reach.

When I was a young man working as a commercial real estate broker, I had the idea of developing an office campus that small business owners could purchase, rather than paying rising rent costs with no equity to show for it. I pitched the idea to several developers, but none would consider it. I considered my situation: I had a mortgage, no "real" money, and my wife was pregnant with twins. I knew the project would work, but I didn't know exactly how. One day I visited an attorney friend who really wanted to own his own office building. I told him I would develop an office campus if he would help finance it. An appraiser friend joined us as partners, and after a great deal of hard work we developed a very successful project.

Over the years, I have attempted numerous ventures, some that succeeded and some that didn't. However, the important principle is that we should prayerfully weigh our options and seek wise counsel, but at some point *take action*. God put it into Nehemiah's heart to return to Jerusalem and rebuild its walls. He spent days fasting and praying about the physical and spiritual condition of the city, and seeking direction from the Lord about how to proceed (Nehemiah 1). Next the king's cupbearer was bold enough to ask for permission to begin the ambitious project. Once he gathered the resources, made the trip, and inspected the walls, Nehemiah challenged everyone with these simple yet powerful words: *". . . I told them of the hand of my God that had been upon me for good, and also of the words that the king had spoken to me. And they said, 'Let us rise up and build.' So they strengthened their hands for the good work."* (Nehemiah 2:18) Of course there were some naysayers who did nothing but try to sabotage the work. That never changes.

The critical point is not the eloquence of Nehemiah's charge, but that a large number people got up and immediately started to work! Some people have a natural propensity to become so overwhelmed with the scope of a project that it paralyzes them—the simplest tasks seem incredibly burdensome. A few are literally sickened by the thought of taking the first step. Others know that God has opened a door, but want just one more sign of assurance. Here's a hard truth—when you know God is leading you to do something, and has made a way for it to happen, you cannot use *anxiety* or *lethargy* as an excuse not to begin. By act of will and obedience you must rise up and put your hands to the good work that is in front of you today. The next day? Do it again. And the next? Do it again. That's how walls get built. What has God put in your heart to do? It's time to get up and take action.

LORD,

Help me to get out of bed today. I am exhausted by what appear to be insurmountable obstacles, personally and nationally. I am overwhelmed by dejection and weariness. I lack energy to do the things I know I must do. Help me, Lord. Restore my faith. I don't know what my efforts will yield, but I know that You are a good God who wants me to get up and do the next right thing. Amen.

UPON REFLECTION

Describe the circumstances or conditions that cause you to procrastinate.

How can you find a healthy middle ground between being impulsive and dawdling?

What is the "next right thing" that is waiting for you to take action?

The first and best victory is to conquer self.

PLATO

EXERCISING ANT-SIZED DISCIPLINE

JAMES DOBSON TOLD a story his mother related about the high school she attended in 1930. The school was located in a small Oklahoma town and it had a terrible football team. They lost most of their games year after year, even to their arch-rival in a nearby community. After one of those big defeats, a wealthy oil man in the community gave a speech to the team and promised every athlete and coach a new car of their choice if they won the next game. Of course the excitement around the school that next week was unmatched. For seven days, the boys ate, drank and breathed football. At night they dreamed about touchdowns. Finally the showdown came. They lost 38 − 0. The team's exuberance and short-term determination did not translate into a single point. Seven days of unbridled excitement and enthusiasm couldn't compensate for the players' lack of discipline, conditioning, practice and study required to to win games.[11] In the same way, many go to the marketplace every day, wishing for a miracle, but settling for mediocrity.

The Scriptures have much to teach about discipline. Have you ever observed the ant? It is absolutely fascinating that God used this small insect to teach an important lesson about diligence. Proverbs 6:6-8 (NLT) says *"Take a lesson from the ants, you lazybones. Learn from their ways and become wise! Though they have no prince or governor or ruler to make them work, they labor hard all summer, gathering food for winter."* The tiny ant instinctively understands the valuable principle that strategic actions today determine your returns tomorrow. The ant perceives the seasons and *plans*—it understands the needs and *prepares.* The ant doesn't wait until the last minute, but shows initiative, organization and consistency. Are you like the ant or the sluggard?

71

Contrast the disciplined ant with the undisciplined worker who has no idea what self-motivation means. These lazy employees must have a bonus dangled in front of them to give an assignment their best. The disciplined professional works hard and smart, not just for the payoff, but the intrinsic reward of working hard with discipline. It's interesting to note that an ant colony has an average life-span of fifteen years, but the individual ant lives only one year on average. In other words, the ant gives its life to something that lasts fifteen times its life-span. Humans have been given lives that average 75 or 80 years with the God-given opportunity to impact eternity. Will you increase your self-discipline accordingly?

LORD,

Thank You for teaching me this important lesson by using a creature that has always seemed insignificant. It reminds me that You use weak things to mystify the "wise." Overcome my desire to look for the easy way out, with thoughts of Your higher purposes for me. Grant me the grace to intentionally implement true diligence in my personal and professional life.

UPON REFLECTION

In what areas of your professional life does your level of disciplined effort fail to match your dreams?

What practical barriers are keeping you from reaching the level of discipline you desire to possess?

What lesson from the ant do you need to add to your work ethic? What is the first step for applying that lesson?

A man's accomplishments in life are the cumulative
effect of his attention to detail.

JOHN FOSTER DULLES

DISTINCTION IN EVERY DETAIL

MICHELANGELO WAS ONCE asked by a friend why he labored so long over the intricate details of the Sistine Chapel in Rome—details so tiny that no one would ever notice. "After all," the friend commented, "who will see whether it is perfect or not?" The artist replied, "God will see." [12] Hundreds of years later, Michelangelo's matchless frescoes, with painstaking attention to detail, are regarded among the greatest works of art ever produced.

God demonstrates artistic excellence beginning with the Creation and continuing to His intricate plans for New Jerusalem (Revelation 21). His supreme originality is found in both design and function. God's Word reveals infinite attention to every detail. Do you do this with your work? Whether you are a big-picture or hands-on person, you should shoot for excellence as you execute both small and large tasks. In today's marketplace, there is a natural temptation just to get by. Minimum standards will not point others to God's magnificence, wonder and power. You were called to ". . . *let your light shine before others, so that they may see your good works and give glory to your Father who is in heaven."* (Matthew 5:16)

Because we were made in God's image, He designed us to be creative, generative workers. *Generative* implies something beyond creativity, the ability to transform. Makoto Fujimura's illustrations for *The Four Holy Gospels* project, commissioned for the four hundredth anniversary of the King James Bible, weren't simply an opportunity to showcase his artistic abilities. I was fortunate enough to see the life-sized paintings when the project was released. In a press conference, he expressed the desire for the images (painted in the ancient Nihonga style) to cause the imagination to be drawn to the deeper truth beyond the words, enabling us to interact with God and be transformed. Fujimura approached his work in the same spirit as many ancient devotional artists. Every stroke he painted was a gift of humble service to God and to the recipients.[13]

A few years ago I observed excellent attention to detail in my own home. When my daughter was engaged to be married, my wife directed the preparations for the wedding. She creatively synthesized Amanda's love for global missions, natural beauty, Asian culture and superb music into a ceremony and reception that was both delightful and God-honoring. What spurred Elaine to consider every detail so thoughtfully? It was her great love and affection for our only daughter. What will motivate you toward more distinctive work? May it be your admiration and gratitude for the heavenly Father, Who is pleased when you have given Him your very best.

LORD,

*Thank You for reminding me that You are the One
I am serving today. Rekindle my desire to bring
innovation and generative creativity to every facet of
my job. As a miniscule part of Your universe,
I am so grateful that You not only notice me but pay
close attention to my life. Let that attribute overflow
to others in my profession today.*

UPON REFLECTION

Are you more big-picture or detail oriented?
When have you seen mediocrity or a neglect of details damage
a project or a business?

Describe how emphasis on quality in small tasks has impacted
a larger project?

Are you more like Michelangelo or his friend?
How can motivation generate the energy for distinction
in your work?

Who does his task from day to day, and meets whatever comes his way,
Being God has willed it so, has found real greatness here below.
For great and low there's but one test: 'tis that each man shall do his best.
Who works with all the strength he can, shall never die in debt to man.

EDGAR GUEST

SIMPLE, BUT PROFOUND

PROVERBS 16 (NLT) is full of simple but profound truths for the market-place. Here are a few of the best:

"We can make our own plans, but the LORD gives the right answer." (16:1)
"People may be pure in their own eyes,
   but the LORD examines their motives." (16:2)
"When people's lives please the LORD, even their enemies are
   at peace with them." (16:7)
"Better to have a little, with godliness, than to be rich
   and dishonest." (16:8)
"How much better to get wisdom than gold,
   and good judgment than silver!" (16:16)
"Pride goes before destruction, and haughtiness before a fall." (16:18)
"Those who listen to instruction will prosper; those who trust the LORD
   will be joyful." (16:20)
"Better to be patient than powerful; better to have self-control than
   to conquer a city." (16:32)

The best way to live is to keep these words close at hand.

Think of the transformation we would see in the marketplace if every man and woman took these proverbs to heart and actually followed them.

Imagine the effect on your city if business owners, government officials, sales people, service workers, technical support and all the rest resolved to entrust their work to God. Proverbs 16:3 (NAS) says, "*Commit your work to the Lord and your plans will be established.*" But is that just a nice sentiment? Do you offer yourself and all of your activities to God every morning? You should because our Father goes to work with you, whether or not you recognize His presence. When I was growing up, my father would assign me jobs like cleaning the garage, mowing the lawn or weeding the flower bed. I remember the effect it had on me when I knew my dad was watching me work. It wasn't that I expected to get in trouble, but seeing him out of the corner of my eye motivated me to give my best effort. I also hoped for his affirmation and approval. Even if you were disappointed or deeply scarred by an unloving or unjust earthly father, your perfect *heavenly* Father longs to show you favor and blessing.

Everyone has been "hard-wired" to desire acceptance and appreciation. God does not withhold praise or affection from those who obey and serve Him. Listen to His announcement to Isaiah: "*Therefore the LORD longs to be gracious to you, And therefore He waits on high to have compassion on You. For the LORD is a God of justice; How blessed are all those who long [wait] for him.*" (Isaiah 30:18, NAS)

You have a higher call to acknowledge that your heavenly Father is present at your workplace. Your occupation is especially important to God, no matter how high or low it is rated by our culture. Today, go make those calls, analyze those numbers, lead your team, type that report, trim that hedge . . . knowing that He is proudly watching you. Tell Him right now that you are doing everything for His fame. That's what we're aiming for. That's answering a higher call. And that's enough for God.

> **LORD,**
>
> *I know You are watching me today, not with*
> *suspicion, but with pleasure. I will be doing my work*
> *to please You. You are more important than*
> *my bosses, associates or clients. Establish and bless*
> *my plans, as I seek to move them so that they*
> *are in line with Yours.*

UPON REFLECTION

When you are honest with yourself, to whom or what have you been committing and dedicating your work?

If someone had been carefully observing your work every day for the last year, whose acceptance and approval would they say is most important to you?

In Proverbs 16:3, we are instructed to dedicate our work to God so our plans will emerge and become established.
Why is the order of those two things significant?

REFLECTING ON
MY JOURNEY

For the first thirty-three years of my life success was easy to define.
For the most part, everything I attempted turned out well, from athletics
to music and drama, to academics (when I worked at it). I played football as
well as leading roles in musicals, entered public speaking contests and led
my youth group. I feared no challenge and was willing to attempt anything.
Everything was possible. Where did this confidence come from?

A handful of influential people shape every person's life. Both of my
parents played an important role in this, but my mom had a special gift
of instilling big dreams and self-assurance in others, especially in me. On
many occasions, she affirmed that God had a calling for my life. I always
felt the freedom to share my aspirations with her without the fear of
criticism. She never communicated doubts about my dreams—becoming
a college quarterback, a Hollywood actor, or even an attorney like Perry
Mason. After parenting my own children, I now wonder why she didn't try
to steer me in more realistic directions. But she didn't. She simply told me
placing my life in God's hands was the key. After a long talk with Mom, I felt
like I could run through a brick wall! Both of my parents modeled a faithful
work and creativity ethic. Into her eighties my mother would often stay
up late arranging music, preparing to teach, or sewing decorations for a
women's conference. That ethos—faithful work and creativity—definitely
spilled over into my life.

After my company went under, I spent almost a year searching my soul to understand what had happened and why. For a performer and perfectionist, swallowing that pill was tough. My friends and critics offered plenty of perspective on our losses. The well intentioned or the cruel commentary did not change the fact that I had sought God, worked hard and still "failed." I remember asking God to reveal what failure was supposed to teach me in a new chapter of life.

Pain teaches lessons slowly. Over time, I've gained some insight. Seeking success centered on self frustrates. Envisioning success centered on God's purposes and service to Him invigorates. Today, I define success as faithfulness to God, not performance or achievement. That definition doesn't stop me from dreaming big. Quite the opposite, my fifties have become the most fulfilling years of my life.

PURSUING
INTEGRITY
IN THE
MARKETPLACE

CULTIVATING A GOOD NAME

BUILDING UNCOMMON CHARACTER

COMPETING IN A CUTTHROAT ENVIRONMENT

IN *THE 7 HABITS OF HIGHLY EFFECTIVE PEOPLE*, Stephen Covey contrasted the difference between what he called personality ethic and character ethic. The personality ethic asserts that success is built on attitude, technique and image, while the character ethic contends that success is built on integrity, courage, compassion and responsibility. Covey observed that after the First World War the criterion for fulfillment in life began to shift from a character-based to a personality-based ethic. Several decades later, the effect of this shift cannot be overstated. As we survey the landscape of today's marketplace, we are suffering a severe drought of godly character. Do not despair, because a call is sounding forth, summoning men and women who have not lost their convictions for a higher standard. By God's gracious hand, an army of workers is rising above compromise and corruption to restore the workplace to an honorable status.

*The poverty of uniqueness is the call of Jesus to
stand alone when the only alternative is to cut a
deal at the price of one's integrity. It is a courageous
determination to make unpopular decisions that are
expressive of the truth of who we are . . .*

BRENNAN MANNING

WHAT'S IN A NAME?

HAVE YOU REFLECTED on your most important assets lately? What you
carry with you to the marketplace is very important. Have you appraised your
resources recently? Your skills, experience, network, financial capital —all
are crucial to your success. However, the Bible mentions something more
important than all of those. Proverbs 22:1, 2 says, *"A good name is to be chosen
rather than great riches, and favor is better than silver or gold. The rich and the poor meet
together; the Lord is the maker of them all."*

This wise saying has strong implications for the way you do your work.
It is staggering to grasp that who we are is more valuable than what we
have. When great wealth and a good name are placed on the scales, God
judges that character carries more weight. In ancient times, a person's name
identified something about their character. Our culture may have underes-
timated the strength of a good name. Our actions and words reveal what is
really in our hearts.

A good name takes many years to forge while fortunes can be won or
lost overnight. Your credibility has more staying power than a brand whose
popularity rises and falls. A good name is your greatest advantage whether
the economy is strong or weak. Reputation is your most powerful asset
whether you own the company or are currently unemployed. A good name
is more valuable than the flash of Donald Trump or the wealth of Bill Gates.

How does one acquire a good name? At the risk of oversimplifying—**do what you say you are going to do over a long period of time**. If you were hoping for a short-cut, there isn't one. Character trumps both charisma and market savvy. It is built by living out a higher standard than most people expect. If you have blown it in the past, making choices you are now ashamed of, don't lose heart or listen to the whispered accusations of the Enemy. Turn around in a new direction and lean on God's mercy. Start doing the right thing today, tomorrow and the next day. By God's grace, in time, a good name can be redeemed.

In a promotionally focused "smoke and mirrors" marketplace, you may feel obliged to promise more than you can actually deliver. You may be tempted to look for loopholes in the novel-length legal documents that have become commonplace. Don't do it. In the name of the One whose good Name is above all other names, I urge you to break ranks with the status quo. Begin building an honorable name that is more than a calling card. *"Therefore God has highly exalted [Jesus] and bestowed on him the name that is above every name, so that at the name of Jesus every knee should bow, in heaven and on earth and under the earth, and every tongue confess that Jesus Christ is Lord, to the glory of God the Father."* (Philippians 2:9-11)

LORD,

I confess that I am easily seduced by the trinkets of success as the world defines it. Help me to genuinely embrace the truth that wealth means nothing without a good name. I want to have a good name because You have given me Your name. Grant me the grace to never again bring dishonor to Your reputation. Give me the resolve to do business Your way, the only way.

UPON REFLECTION

How are people making a name for themselves in opposition to what this proverb teaches?
When have you fallen into this trap?

How is a good name different from a good image?

On a scale of 1 to 10, what value have you given to a good name?
What immediate action will you take to address your reputation and credibility?

*We're not necessarily doubting that God will do
the best for us; we are wondering how painful
the best will turn out to be.*

C.S. LEWIS

CHARACTER TRUMPS LOGIC

THE SCORPION, a very poor swimmer, asked a turtle to carry him across the river. "Are you mad?" exclaimed the turtle. "You'll sting me while I'm swimming, and I'll drown." "My dear turtle," laughed the scorpion, "if I were to sting you, you would drown and I would go down with you. Now, where is the logic in that?" "You're right!" cried the turtle. "Hop on!" The scorpion climbed aboard and halfway across the river gave the turtle a sting. As they both began to sink to the bottom, with a sigh the turtle inquired, "Do you mind if I ask you something? You said there'd be no logic in stinging me, so why did you do it?" "It has nothing to do with logic," the drowning scorpion replied. "It's just my character." [14]

As much as I hate to admit it, character trumps logic. Nowhere is this reality made clearer than in the marketplace. For instance, it is reasonable to assume that taking advantage of a client to close a deal will undermine your future business association, yet we are tempted to choose the most expedient approach to get what we want at the moment. Character trumps logic. We might recognize that employees will lose all respect for us if we drive them to burnout, but if we procrastinate on a project, we may manipulate employees to complete it for us. Character trumps logic. A high level of performance may carry you for a time, but ultimately your true character will be revealed and could cost you dearly.

Character is the sum of your current values [ethics, morals, ideals]. Character is your true nature when no one is looking. Your inner makeup is exposed when you are mistreated or your idea is blocked. Honesty, diligence, unselfishness, patience, self-discipline, humility, perseverance and wisdom are essential qualities the workplace desperately needs. I can hear the cry of Psalm 12:1-2 rising up from the marketplace, "*Save, O LORD, for the godly one is gone; for the faithful have vanished from among the children of man. Everyone utters lies to his neighbor; with flattering lips and double heart they speak.*" Don't misunderstand. I am not without hope and can testify of many men and women whose Christ-like character shines brightly within their company or industry. On the other hand, it is time for the gaps in our character to be filled. This will not happen by attending a business ethics seminar. The source of godly character is God, the only perfect model to emulate. God is righteous and just, yet merciful, with never-ending love expressed by kindness. The Bible records several hundred names for God, each revealing a different facet of His character. God has a plan in place to make us like Himself, but we have a role to play as well (2 Peter 1:3-8).

Character building can transform the marketplace over a long period of time, but it starts with individuals who follow a steady diet of reading, meditating, and applying God's Word to every area of life. Romans 12:1-2 (NLT) sums it up in a practical way: "*And so dear brothers and sisters, I plead with you to give your bodies to God because of all he has done for you. Let them be a living and holy sacrifice—the kind he will find acceptable. This is truly the way to worship him. Don't copy the behavior and customs of this world, but let God transform you into a new person by changing the way you think. Then you will know God's will for you, which is good and pleasing and perfect.*" That's a promise you can trust.

LORD,

*I see the gaps in my character. When everyone else
sees the good, I know the flaws and shortcomings
just beneath the surface. I need You to change me
and build Your character in me. I realize this is not
a short term proposition, but I am ready for You
to etch Your values into my soul. Let Your Word do
its work in me, and show me that Your will is the
ultimate pleasure in life and work.*

UPON REFLECTION

When has your character trumped logic during the last year?

How often must you "go against the grain" of your workplace
to maintain your values?

In what area are you most vulnerable to compromising your
integrity in your particular profession?
How are you guarding against that temptation?

*Never sacrifice the permanent on the altar
of the immediate.*

TIM KIMMEL

SELLING OUT

HOW OFTEN HAVE you been in the midst of a discussion about a proposed venture or business deal only to hear the question, "But what is the
bottom line?" If you hope to survive in the competitive marketplace, you
must learn the importance of cutting to the chase. Mary Pipher summed it
up pretty well in *Writing to Change the World*: "In the world of business, all of
life is boiled down to one word: profit."[15]

One day, Jesus was dialoguing with some folks, and asked the ultimate
bottom line question: *"And what do you benefit if you gain the whole world but lose your
own soul? Is anything worth more than your soul?"* (Matthew 16:26, NLT) This is
a question we should regularly ask ourselves. The marketplace constantly
teases us with the "whole world." Playing by the rules of the corporate
world ("Do whatever it takes and look out for number one,") promises the
chance to climb to the top. Few stop long enough to ask if the *whole world* is
worth what it will cost to obtain.

In John Grisham's bestselling novel and movie, *The Rainmaker*, the inexpe-
rienced lawyer Rudy Baylor (Matt Damon) went against the ruthless lawyer
Leo Drummond (Jon Voight). In the middle of a deposition, Rudy asked
Leo a jaw-dropping question: "Do you remember when you first sold out?"
Every day you walk into your place of business, you are in danger of doing
just that. As Jesus warned, we must pay closer attention to our souls.

Let's start with defining a *healthy soul*. Our soul [psyche, heart, core],
when connected with God, results in wholesome thoughts, accurate
judgments, balanced emotions, honorable motivations and wise choices.

A healthy soul is anchored in biblical truth rather than cultural opinion, unbridled compulsion, stubborn arrogance or insecurity (rooted in fear). A healthy soul is at liberty to engage in daily responsibilities and activities with steady confidence and complete fulfillment.

Of course your business must make a profit. It all comes down to your motives and your process for pursuing them. In *Business for the Glory of God*, Wayne Grudem wrote "The ability to earn a profit results in multiplying our resources while helping other people. It is a wonderful ability that God gave us and it is not evil or morally neutral, but is fundamentally good." [16] Are you protecting your soul? Are you guarding your heart? Go for the bottom line, fully maximizing your God-given strengths and opportunities. Ultimately, you *are* called to sell out—not to selfish gain—but to Jesus Christ and His coming kingdom.

LORD,

Thank You for warning me about selling out my

loyalty to You in order to acquire things.

Help my love for You increase, and my lust for the

temporary to decrease. As the psalmist prayed,

"Keep my soul." Protect me from the seduction

I will encounter today. Give me the compassion

and kindness of Christ, and grant me Your favor

as I work according to Your character.

UPON REFLECTION

In what specific ways does the bottom line within your business bump up against the biblical values you want to follow?

What would constitute selling out in your profession?

What is the most important step you need to take that will lead to a healthier soul?

The power of Satan is presenting the lie.
The power of the believer is in knowing the truth.

NEIL ANDERSON

RECOGNIZING THE REAL DEAL

HOW DOES A BANKER keep counterfeit currency out of his cash drawers? One way is to teach the tellers how to distinguish between genuine and counterfeit bills. Experts say the secret to recognizing counterfeit money is not looking at endless examples of phony bills, but intensive exposure to the *real thing*. Once the characteristics of genuine currency can be recognized, a counterfeit bill will clearly stand out.[17] This principle also holds true in life and the marketplace. We are all capable of being deceived—it happens all the time. We hire people who appear to possess superstar characteristics only to find out they weren't competent or trustworthy. We bite on a deal that seems too good to be true, and ultimately realize that it was. We change vendors based on pledged promises only to discover that they couldn't deliver what they guaranteed. It is bad enough to be disappointed, but to be hoodwinked is even worse.

Has a leader charmed you into full support then taken advantage of you? Has a respected mentor misled you with harmful teaching? Has an employer betrayed you after promising a promotion? Dishonesty is as old as the crafty serpent who presented Eve the opportunity of a lifetime: *"But I am afraid that as the serpent deceived Eve by his cunning, your thoughts will be led astray from a sincere and pure devotion to Christ."* (2 Corinthians 11:3) Paul went on to warn that it should not surprise us that so-called Christians may mislead us: *"For such [people] are false apostles, deceitful workmen, disguising themselves as apostles of Christ. And no wonder, for even Satan disguises himself as an angel of light."* (11:13-14)

Try not to become cynical or expect an evil spirit on every corner, but saturate [inundate, oversupply] your mind with the truth. Pray for greater discernment then surround yourself with like-minded people who consistently display those qualities. You will distinguish those who aim to serve from those who try to swindle . . . most of the time. Jesus instructed his disciples that you can't always judge by outward appearance. *"'Beware of false prophets, who come to you in sheep's clothing but inwardly are ravenous wolves. You will recognize them by their fruits. Are grapes gathered from thornbushes, or figs from thistles? So, every healthy tree bears good fruit, but the diseased tree bears bad fruit.'"* (Matthew 7:15-17)

It's all about the fruit, which means it might take some time to observe whether someone's character is genuine or counterfeit. Who are you surrounding yourself with today? Would others bear witness of your authenticity? Have you set your mind on the truth flowing from Scripture?

LORD,

Thank You that I am not left to wander in an aimless

sea of relativity and non-absolutes in the world

I live and work in. Thank You for revealing spiritual

reality to me and for inviting me to be a part of Your

Kingdom of light—a whole new way of life that

is centered in truth. Lord, thank You most of all

that truth is more than a set of statements in a book.

Truth can be seen in a person, and His name

is Jesus Christ.

UPON REFLECTION

As you reflect on your past, when were you deceived into believing something that wasn't true?

In terms of authentic godliness, how would you rate the influences around you the majority of the time?

In your industry or workplace, how can you differentiate between the genuine and the counterfeit?

The Christian ideal has not been tried and found wanting; it has been found difficult and left untried.

G.K. CHESTERTON

WHAT ARE THEY SAYING ABOUT YOU?

IT'S NOT EASY being a public figure. Just ask Martha Stewart or Roger Clemens or Governor Rod Blagojevich. The press is always looking for a juicy story, especially when a high profile person steps out of line—the more personal and humiliating the better. Thanks to social media, it only takes minutes to spread information—or misinformation—around the world.

On a more positive note, Tony Dungy, a former NFL coach, is a worthy example of a public figure that uses his influence for good. Dungy led the Indianapolis Colts to the playoffs ten years in a row, and became the first African American coach to win a Super Bowl (2007). He experienced success and notoriety as an athlete, then a coach, but one columnist wrote that Tony Dungy is a *better person* than he is a coach. Another commented that on a scale of 1 – 10, he would give Dungy an 11. The New York Times declared "Dungy will be remembered for being a man of grace and quiet forcefulness."[18] And these are not eulogies! Tony Dungy has always been open but not obnoxious about his faith in Christ. The title of his first book, Quiet Strength, opens a window into his character. The way he has conducted himself as a man, a husband, a father, a coach and a humanitarian has made a powerful impression nationwide.

Another public figure lived 2,500 years ago, before newspapers, television or the internet. Daniel was a teen when he was deported from his homeland but set himself apart by his excellence, integrity and faith. Over the years, Daniel proved to be a loyal and wise leader. As his professional career developed, the Babylonian king appointed him to a strategic administrative role. "Then this Daniel became distinguished above all the other high officials and satraps, because an excellent spirit was in him. And the king planned to set him over the whole kingdom. Then the [others] sought to find a ground for complaint or any fault, because he was faithful, and no error or fault was found in him." (Daniel 6:3-4)

Neither Tony Dungy nor Daniel exemplifies perfection, but both of their lives display God-honoring character. Few of us will become famous, yet we work in a public domain where neighbors, friends, associates and other impressionable people watch us. What do you suppose people are saying about you?

FATHER,

I am so thankful for men like Tony Dungy and many
others who have lived out their convictions in very
difficult arenas and gut-wrenching circumstances.
This is both encouraging and challenging.
I know people are watching me, and though I don't
want to become motivated by men's praise,
I do want my life to please You and point others
in Your direction. I cannot live this kind of life
without Your intervention, transformation, and
protection. Help me live faithfully over the long haul
like Your servants Dungy and Daniel.

UPON REFLECTION

Describe an error in judgment that you made impulsively but could not take back. What did you learn from that?

If you surveyed your co-workers, clients or customers what might they say about your reputation, both positively and negatively? Would they guess that you are a Christian?

Knowing the legacy you would like to leave, what character qualities do you need to address?

The buck stops here.

PRESIDENT HARRY TRUMAN

THE OWNERSHIP OF RESPONSIBILITY

T. BOONE PICKENS said his favorite joke is about a banker who called in an oil man to review his loans. The banker said, "We let you borrow a million dollars to drill new wells, and they were all dry holes." The oil man said, "Well, it could have been worse." The banker continued, "Then we let you have another million dollars to get some new drilling equipment and all of it broke down." The oil man said, "Well, it could have been worse." That's when the banker said, "I'm tired of hearing you say, 'It could have been worse.' How could it have been worse?" The oil man said, "Well, it could have been my *money*."[19] Our culture reinforces a dangerous trend of avoiding responsibility for actions. The political arena is filled with annoying sounds of the blame game. More energy is spent on blaming others for what goes wrong than accepting responsibility and taking action to solve the problem. The litigation industry (can I say that?) has flourished as a result of this mindset. If the stock price, market share, profit margin or return on investment drops, just watch the fingers point. We need to learn how to take ownership when the finger points to us.

Jesus told a difficult story about a wealthy business owner who had a manager charged with squandering his opportunities and responsibilities. (Luke 16:1-13) The proprietor called his manager in and said to him, "*. . . What is this that I hear about you? Turn in the account of your management, for you can no longer be manager.*" (Luke 16:2) Whether or not we admit it, everyone is accountable at some level. People who have difficulty confessing that they are wrong already feel shame over some inadequacy. If you are a CEO, a manager or a leader in any capacity, you know that employees pay close attention to your actions. They are watching your attitudes and whether you have the courage to admit your mistakes and shortcomings. If you will set a tone of humility, your entire work environment can be enhanced. The weight of personal failings is difficult to handle. Pretending to be perfect just perpetuates the illusion that there are any perfect people. Wake up from this fantasy. *"There is none righteous, not even one."* (Romans 3:10, NAS [quotes Psalm 14; Psalm 53])

Only one human being ever took *ultimate* responsibility, carrying the sin of the world on His back all the way to the Cross. If you have trusted in Jesus' sacrifice and experienced God's forgiveness there is no reason to hide from the truth that people make mistakes—at home and in the marketplace. If sales are down in your company, bring everyone together, acknowledge your accountability in the matter, and begin working on solutions. If you know you made an error, don't try to bury it; speak up and correct your blunder. How else will your integrity be demonstrated?

"One who is faithful in very little is also faithful in much, and one who is dishonest in a very little is also dishonest in much. If then you have not been faithful in the unrighteous wealth, who will entrust to you the true riches? And if you have not been faithful in that which is another's, who will give you that which is your own? No servant can serve two masters, for either he will hate the one and love the other, or he will be devoted to the one and despise the other. You cannot serve God and money." (Luke 16:10-13) You serve your employer and protect your company's interests by admitting when you are wrong, seeking to make things right, learning new lessons and moving forward. This may not be the norm in your workplace, but it is the way God designed life to be in His kingdom.

LORD,

I confess my pattern of making excuses for all of my troubles. I tend to look for the weaknesses of others rather than admitting my own incompetence. Give me the courage to accept responsiblity for my own actions and attitudes, knowing that Your love, forgiveness, and acceptance is my true confidence and most cherished gift. Give me the grace to set that kind of tone in my workplace.

UPON REFLECTION

Why is it easier to identify the flaws of others rather than your own?

How have the great leaders you have observed addressed their inadequacies and shortcomings?
What can you learn from your observations?

What neglected shortcoming or failure (professionally or personally), do you need to take responsibility for?
What action is required to do this?

An unguarded strength and an unprepared heart
are double weaknesses.

GORDON MACDONALD

DEFENDING YOUR AIRSPACE

YEARS AGO, the Russian military was humiliated in a most unusual way. A small airplane landed in Red Square in the heart of Moscow. It was unimaginable that this could happen since airspace was restricted and the air defense system made territorial violation impossible for miles around the city. The military was certain that no intruder could ever make it into Moscow, much less Red Square—but then a little plane circled the area, then landed right next to the Kremlin Wall and Lenin's Tomb. Mathias Rust got out and began to sign autographs in the area once considered the most secure in the world. The world was amused, the Russian government was embarrassed, and the German pilot was elated to pull off such an amazing feat![20]

When you feel the strongest, you may be the most at risk. There are many stories of cities that claimed to be impregnable, then were captured by surprise. In the same way, proud leaders have been conquered, believing they were unstoppable. King David was said to be a man after God's own heart. He had defeated giants, kings and assassins for the glory of God, yet he fell into temptation that led to adultery and murder. When Jesus foretold that all of his disciples would fall away because of His crucifixion, Peter argued, *"Though they all fall away because of you, I will never fall away"* (Matthew 26:31-35) . . . famous last words. Hours later, Peter panicked, lost his courage and denied Christ three times.

Can you identify the most vulnerable areas of your heart, the most susceptible parts? It's difficult to detect your own blind spots (that's why they are called "blind spots.") We are keenly aware of some weaknesses, but many blind spots are connected to our *strengths*. For example, you may be good at handling money, so financial holdings give you a sense of security. Don't ignore Proverbs 18:11, *"A rich man's wealth is his strong city, and like a high wall in his imagination."* You might take pride in the perfect family or high standing in the business community, professional expertise or great generosity. Our strong suits are often left exposed because we didn't heed Paul's warning to the Corinthians: *"Therefore let anyone who thinks that he stands take heed lest he fall."* (1 Corinthians 10:12) No one's airspace is invincible.

How do you protect against a spiritual ambush? First you must accept the possibility that you are capable of the worst personal failures. There is no area of life where you are immune from compromise or ruin. Because all are sinners, we must stay on guard at all times. Second, you must increase your sensitivity to the Holy Spirit's guidance and warnings. That is why a daily time of reflection on Scripture and response to God is indispensable. Thankfully God's mercy and grace can cover your worst failures. Don't drop your head in shame, but instead turn away from your wrongdoing toward God and go a new way. Saturate your heart with the stories of David's and Peter's restoration and how both of them finished strong.

If you think "I haven't fallen that far," be careful and remember Red Square. The tiniest crack in a foundation can destroy the tallest building. Instead ask God to reveal your blind spots. As you become exceedingly aware of your shortcomings, God's grace will surround your airspace when you call out to Him in dependence during each new day.

LORD,

The farther I travel down the path You have

set before me, the more I realize that You have

graciously protected me even when I wasn't aware.

You've alerted me to my extreme vulnerability.

Do not let me wander from Your truth. Guard

my heart from complacency and keep me humbly

clinging to You. Prepare my heart for the tests

and temptations waiting around the next corner,

and grant me the will to place all of my confidence

in Your grace.

UPON REFLECTION

What person's moral failure has had the greatest impact on you?

Describe an experience where you were caught off guard, thinking your "airspace" was inpenetrable, only to be proven wrong?

One of the key strategies for protecting your character is to incorporate more accountability in your professional and personal life. What steps are needed for you to employ this strategy?

Blessed is the Christian whose life is so transparent,
who is trustworthy and neither corrupt nor
negligent, so that the only way he or she can be
destroyed is by making Christian conduct and
conviction a crime.

D. A. CARSON

LIVING ABOVE REPROACH

GOLF LEGEND BOBBY JONES is considered by some the greatest golfer who ever played the game, yet as a young man Jones struggled with a terrible temper—his nickname was "Club Thrower." A retired golf pro recognized Jones' talent and his character flaw. The pro once told him, "Bobby, you are good enough to win that tournament, but you'll never win until you can control that temper of yours. You miss a shot—you get upset—and then you lose." Over the next several years Jones learned to control his temper. His mentor later stated, "Bobby was fourteen when he mastered the game of golf, but he was twenty-one when he mastered himself." He went on to become a model of sportsmanship and character.[21]

It seems that celebrities and leaders disappoint us with integrity breeches and moral compromises on a daily basis. It's easy for the seeds of cynicism and disillusionment to take root—especially if we know the offender personally. Do you really count on the truthfulness of what a candidate tells the media? Do your employer's actions line up with his or her commentary? Let's face it; the marketplace is screaming for professionals of true character, who live their lives and do their work with excellence, integrity and faith. How can you identify a person's true character? Is anyone above criticism or accusation? I read about a man who prospered in his workplace with great honor. He was successful, wealthy and possessed an impeccable international reputation. He also had time for his large family. The Bible describes Job as " . . . *blameless and upright, one who feared God and turned away from evil.*" (Job 1:1) When Satan came before the Lord (intending to cause trouble, no doubt), God went a step farther, "*Have you considered my servant Job, that there is none like him on the earth . . .?*" (1:8)

Job's character was beyond reproach even after God gave Satan permission to test the motivation behind his faith. Job's confidence in God endured incomprehensible adversity and rejection by his closest friends, as well as a season of searching for answers and questioning God. In the end, Job confessed to God, "*I know that you can do all things, and that no purpose of yours can be thwarted. 'Who is this that hides counsel without knowledge?' Therefore I have uttered what I did not understand, things too wonderful for me, which I did not know. 'Hear and I will speak; I will question you, and you make it known to me.' I had heard of you by hearing of the ear, but now my eye sees you; therefore I despise myself and repent in dust and ashes.*" (Job 42:1-6) After losing everything he owned, including his family, his health and his support system, Job was finally exonerated by God. His self-righteous friends were punished for accusing him of dishonesty. Job's faith was actually *solidified* through his trials and sufferings. He demonstrated for us that Satan will never have the last word in a true believer's story.

During the final play-off of a U.S. Open tournament, Bobby Jones's ball ended up in a rough just off the fairway. As he set up to play his shot, he accidentally caused his ball to move. He immediately turned to the marshals and announced the foul. The marshals discussed the situation among themselves. They hadn't seen the ball move. Neither did anyone in the gallery. They left it up to Jones whether to take the penalty stroke, which he did. Later, when a marshal commended Jones on his high level of integrity, Jones replied, "Do you commend a bank robber for not robbing a bank? No, you don't. This is how the game of golf should be played at all times." Jones lost the match that day—by one stroke. But he didn't lose his integrity. His character was so well-known that the United States Golf Association's sportsmanship award came to be named the Bob Jones Award.[22] What will be the end of your story?

LORD,

I long to live an honorable life, yet sometimes that seems out of my reach. I ask for Your grace to move ahead with confidence in Your purifying work on my soul. Turn the things I know to be right into convictions—not just preferences. By Your grace, I ask that I may become a person whose enemies are unable to find "corruption or negligence" in my life or work. I submit myself to Your will and ways in my life and trust that despite any testing Your name will be honored throughout all my days on Earth.

UPON REFLECTION

What person comes to mind when you use the phrase "beyond reproach?" Describe why.

No one is perfect, but what does living and working with Job's kind of character look like in practice?

Which of the following provides your greatest motivation for maintaining integrity? Explain.

Fear of getting caught?

Concern about letting someone down?

Hope of propelling you to success?

Because it's the right thing to do? Other?

*If anyone would like to acquire humility, I can,
I think, tell him the first step. The first step is
to realize that one is proud.*

C.S. LEWIS

REVOLUTIONARY PRINCIPLE OR ANCIENT TRUTH?

THE MARKETPLACE HAS a way of bullying us. It's not what is said, but all the unwritten rules like "You have to take what is yours" and "Nice guys finish last." Jim Collins wrote the bestselling book, *Good to Great*, which exposed another alleged truth: "It takes a big ego to lead your company to the top." Using very strenuous, yet black-and-white statistical criteria, Collins identified eleven companies that rose from being good to **great** companies. One of the distinguishing characteristics of each was what the author referred to as "Level 5 Leadership". Collins wrote, "We were surprised, shocked really, to discover the type of leadership required for turning a good company into a great one. Compared to high-profile leaders with big personalities who make headlines and become celebrities, the good-to-great leaders seem to have come from Mars. Self-effacing, quiet, reserved, even shy—these leaders are a paradoxical blend of personal humility and professional will."[23]

This struck readers as an amazing phenomenon, a revolutionary idea and a new management technique; but students of the Bible have been taught the virtue of humility for over two thousand years:

> "You younger men, likewise, be subject to your elders; and all of you, clothe yourselves with humility toward one another, for GOD IS OPPOSED TO THE PROUD, BUT GIVES GRACE TO THE HUMBLE. Therefore humble yourselves under the mighty hand of God, that He may exalt you at the proper time . . ." (1 Peter 5:5-6, NAS)

"So, as those who have been chosen of God, holy and beloved, put on a heart of compassion, kindness, humility, gentleness and patience . . ." (Colossians 3:12, NAS)

"Have this mind among yourselves, which is yours in Christ Jesus who, though he was in the form of God, did not count equality with God a thing to be grasped, but made himself nothing, taking the form of a servant, being born in the likeness of men. And being found in human form, he humbled himself by becoming obedient to the point of death, even death on a cross." (Philippians 2:5-8)

Jesus sets the standard for the marketplace. Jim Collins correctly identified a crucial characteristic of effective leaders, but the Scriptures reveal the heart and mind of God on the matter. We don't have to leave humility at church and put on arrogance at work to succeed. Cultural trends may change with the wind, but God's Word will last forever (Isaiah 40:8). This is not to minimize the tension between modesty and promotion of your company, product or service. The sweet spot is found in clarifying that God is God and you are at His service. You honor Him by respectfully and unassumingly serving your associates, clients, patients or customers day by day. What kind of leader are you—good or great? Ask God as you stop to take a good look in the mirror.

LORD,

You have given me the roadmap not only to find You but to discover Your leadership principles for the marketplace. It's true. Your ways are so much better than my ways. If You will lead me, I will follow Your timeless strategy. Give me the guts to live as close to the truth as possible. I acknowledge that apart from You, I can do nothing. I celebrate that with You, I can do all that You have ordained.

UPON REFLECTION

Why are big egos and conceit so prominent in today's marketplace?

What is the difference between confidence and arrogance?

How can a professional remain humble while effectively advertising and advancing their product or service?
In what ways will you seek to improve this balance?

*In the Christian life, it's not how you start that
matters. It's how you finish.*

STEVE FARRAR

HITTING THE WALL

FOR MOST OF my adult life, basketball was my sport of choice; but I finally
had to "retire" due to cumulative nagging injuries. Although I was never
a serious runner, I often ran to stay in shape. After watching my father go
through two knee replacements, I decided it was wiser to become a walker.
My competitive nature still needed a challenge, so I determined to walk
a marathon—besides how much training could it take to "just walk?" It
didn't take long to figure out that walking twenty-six miles takes a lot of
focused training.

One dynamic in marathons is hitting the wall—the point where you believe you cannot go on. I was told that this could happen, so I prepared
myself for the possibility. The Music City Marathon began and I got off to
a good start. My goal was six hours (about 14 minutes/mile). I reached the
halfway point at three hours, and stayed on pace until mile twenty-one . . .
when I hit the wall. My legs got tight and I was aching all over. I felt light-
headed and my body screamed "Stop!" Fortunately, I had already decided
that nothing was going to defeat me, so I turned up my iPod, put my head
down and pressed on. By mile twenty-four, I began to get my second wind
and knew I was going to finish after all. I even did a little running during
the last mile, hoping to hit my time. In the end, I missed my goal by a few
minutes, but learned what marathons are all about—finishing.

Business and a life of faith are about finishing, and perseverance will
help you accomplish that goal. Everyone will eventually hit the wall, perhaps many times. Your wall may be a ruined partnership or a wounded

relationship. Your promising new venture may leave you fighting for your professional life. Perhaps you are nose-to-nose with a financial crisis or a job that you hate. Hitting the wall may sound like a trite analogy until you have encountered the paralysis that tempts you to give up, settle, quit—or put your head down and push on through to the finish.

Perseverance is the pre-determined decision to *never quit what is begun until the purpose has been fulfilled.* It is the will to press on even when circumstances are working against you. Determination is an attribute of God, thus a character quality worthy of cultivation. God is a marathoner—He will perfect the faith He began in you. Hebrews 12 is one of the most encouraging chapters in the Bible because it challenges us to "*[Look] to Jesus, the founder and perfecter of our faith, who for the joy that was set before him, endured the cross, despising the shame, and is seated at the right hand of the throne of God.*" (12:2) Regardless of how weak or fragile your faith may be, God will help you persevere through a project, a contract, a partnership or a marriage. If you have hit the wall in any area of life today, you are not alone. "*Therefore, do not throw away your confidence, which has a great reward. For you have need of endurance, so that when you have done the will of God, you may receive what was promised.*" (Hebrews 10:35-36, NAS)

LORD,

I need You to change my perspective when I feel like
I can't go another step in life. Help me to see Your
pathway to the finish line and to keep my eyes on
Jesus, who never gave up and is already reigning over
His coming kingdom. Teach me to rely on
Your adequacy and sufficiency in all my affairs.
Because You are committed to finish what You started
in me, empower me to finish what You have called me
to do today.

UPON REFLECTION

Describing your life as a topographical map, what kind of terrain would best describe your journey over the last year (flat, rocky, mountainous, hilly, steep slopes, deep valleys)? Explain.

What are the primary factors that determine whether a person gives up or endures?

In what areas of your personal and professional life do you find it most challenging to persevere rather than quit? Explain why.

He must increase, but I must decrease.

JOHN THE BAPTIST

WHAT YOU BRING TO THE TABLE

AS A YOUNG developer in my twenties, I was blessed to be involved in a number of deals that were both successful and profitable. Before I knew it, I found myself competing with powerful companies and individuals for "higher level" projects. I remember the tension between inwardly wrestling with my inexperience and outwardly displaying the confident image necessary for a serious player in the marketplace. I will never forget certain meetings with highly-regarded attorneys and heavy-hitters in the real estate investment arena—those experiences were simultaneously exhilarating and terrifying!

At those meetings, the same phrase was repeated verbally or nonverbally. Everyone's lingering question was *"What are you bringing to the table?"* Like a high stakes poker game, each person would eventually show their cards. Did they have an inside relationship with the tenant or buyer? Was it the idea or the deal itself? Perhaps it was the capital or financial leverage. Sometimes it was a particular skill. The bottom line was always this: If you want to come to the table, you'd better bring something of value.

John 3:27 has a way of bringing us back to earth. *". . . A person cannot receive even one thing unless it is given him from heaven."* Could this be the "chill pill" that alleviates your anxiety today? God is the source for anything of table value that you possess. You are responsible for sharpening the skills, multiplying the network and maximizing the resources. Of course, He calls you to hard work and quality development as well as marketable skills and resources. Ultimately, though, God is the giver of everything you have to offer your industry.

As I prepare to tackle new assignments where I will be competing with others, I still find myself reviewing the things I have learned over the last thirty-five years. I still ask, "What am I bringing to the table?" I already know the two-sided answer: in one sense I bring **nothing**. Nothing that wasn't handed to me for God's supreme purposes. In another sense, I bring **everything**. Wherever I go, and whomever I encounter, I possess something priceless—God Himself is operating through me. I share His presence, light, strength, wisdom, and hope, to name a few. With that, I can realistically compete. What are you bringing to the table?

LORD GOD,

I have responsibilities and expectations pressing in
on me today. I feel the unending pressure to produce
results that keep me indispensable in my workplace.
Thank You for never leaving me on my own, and for
reminding me that I have more than myself to bring
to the table. You will give me everything I need as I
depend on You as my most valuable asset today.
Now I'm ready to face anything!

UPON REFLECTION

In human terms, what do you bring to the table in your type of work?

How much are you depending on your skills and resources versus God's influence and provision?

How will you practically work toward the right balance between completely trusting God and continuing to sharpen skills?

Competition is fundamentally good and provides
many opportunities for glorifying God, but also
many temptations to sin.

WAYNE GRUDEM

CAUGHT UP IN THE HEAT OF COMPETITION

CHARLES SCHWAB, the American industrialist and steel industry leader, had a steel mill manager whose men were not producing their quota. Schwab challenged the manager: "How can a man as capable as you not make this mill turn out the way it should?" "I don't know," the manager replied, "I have coaxed them and pushed them, but nothing works. They just will not produce." This conversation took place at the end of the day just before the night shift began. Schawb said, "Give me a piece of chalk," then turned to the nearest man and asked, "How many heats did your shift make today?" "Six." Without another word Schwab wrote a "6" on the floor and walked away. When the night shift came in they saw the "6" and asked what it meant. "The big boss was in here today," the men said. "He asked how many heats we made and chalked it out on the floor." The next morning Schwab walked through the mill again. The night shift had rubbed out the "6" and replaced it with a big "7". The day shift went about its production, determined to show the night shift that "7" was not all that remarkable. That evening they left an impressive "10" on the floor. In short order, the mill which was lagging behind in production was turning out more work than any other plant. "The way to get things done," said Schwab, "is to stimulate competition. I don't mean in a sordid money-getting way, but the desire to excel."[24]

We are all quite familiar with the intense competition of the marketplace. On some level, everyone competes for orders, customers, market share, ideas or clients. There is a contest inside a company and outside. Some people view competition as an evil concept—a part of commerce that creates bad motives and behavior. We have certainly observed abuses during the heat of rivalry—a killer-like instinct between business counterparts, win-at-any-cost attitudes, or envy and jealousy that lead to a compromise of values. However, competition is neither evil nor good, in and of itself. Competition is a reality that God will use to bring glory to Himself when we perform as He designed.

Competition should spur you toward greater excellence and increase your desire to improve and grow. Ecclesiastes 4:4 (NAS) says, *"I have seen that every labor and every skill which is done is the result of rivalry between a man and his neighbor . . ."* The Hebrew word for "rivalry" (qin'ah) can have a negative or positive moral connotation. In this context, it merely conveys its existence without any judgment. When you observe what others have accomplished, you should become motivated to hone your own skills and work smarter. Paul used an athletic competition to describe his commitment to self-discipline and victory: *"Do you not know that in a race all the runners run, but only one receives the prize? So run that you may obtain it. Every athlete exercises self-control in all things. They do it to receive a perishable wreath, but we an imperishable. So I do not run aimlessly; I do not box as one beating the air. But I discipline my body and keep it under control lest after preaching to others I myself should be disqualified."* (1 Corinthians 9:24-27, NAS) This same dynamic carries over into business. Through healthy competition, many positive things have been generated—creativity, ingenuity, ethical policies, quality products, lower prices and new jobs. Consider all the ways that God can use the competition within your business to shape you and allow others to admire Him.

LORD,

*I have watched how You have used my competitive juices
to keep me striving toward greater achievements personally
and professionally. You have used a "challenge" as a tool
to move me out of complacency and into action. At the same
time, I sometimes allow the spirit of competition to lead to
resentment and covetousness. Grant me the wisdom to know
how to channel my competitive spirit for Your triumphs
rather than my own. Help Your followers throughout
the marketplace spur each other toward a healthier, more
constructive approach that will make non-believers
take notice.*

UPON REFLECTION

What negative effects can competition produce?

How is God using competition to propel you toward greater excellence?

What key principles will guide you toward a healthier attitude toward your business rivals?

A competitive world has two possibilities for you.
You can lose. Or, if you want to win, you can change.

LESTER C. THUROW,
DEAN, SLOAN SCHOOL OF MANAGEMENT, MIT

FACING THE DEMANDS OF CHANGE

IN 1929, Martin Van Buren, the governor of New York, was deeply concerned about a new form of transportation known as the railroad. Convinced that it would cause widespread unemployment among those who worked to run the canal boat system, he wrote to President Andrew Jackson presenting his case for why the railroads must be stopped.

"As you may know, Mr. President, railroad carriages are pulled at the enormous speed of 15 miles per hour by engines which, in addition to endangering life and limb of passengers, roar and snort their way through the countryside, setting fire to crops, scaring the livestock, and frightening women and children. The Almighty certainly never intended that people should travel at such breakneck speed."[25]

In light of the great changes in transportation since the time that letter was penned, you might consider his perspective humorous and woefully short-sighted. Yet when we are honest, most of us tend to resist change.

As you consider the impact of global competition on the marketplace, your profession and your family, one of the most obvious results is change, whether positive or negative. Competition not only stimulates a strong work ethic and keeps companies on their toes, but it also demands change that can lead to creative, helpful, even life-saving innovations. Today, I own a lightweight wireless tablet that is amazingly faster than the first computer I bought in 1991 for $2,400. It has features I couldn't imagine back then, and at one-fourth of the cost. We like those kinds of changes, but what about the flip side? What is taxing or stressful about the continual demand to change?

Competition means that some businesses simply will not make it. Progress in technology may phase out your occupation. Global commerce may entice your children to move away. Over time, an individual or company that stands still too long will be surpassed. Constant adjustment and growth are necessary for success. You can choose to adapt willingly or reluctantly, but you can't stay the same. Flexibility and an eye for new possibilities take a God-sized perspective. Think about it this way: the entire universe has been designed for seasons, migration and growth. Small seeds become blooming flowers and towering trees. Ideas build on each other from the wheel to the car to the rocket to the space station to—what next? Philippians 1:6 (MSG) promises that things will continue to change, but *"There has never been the slightest doubt in my mind that the God who started this great work in you would keep at it and bring it to a flourishing finish on the very day Christ Jesus appears."* Try to view competition as your friend, not your adversary. Live with expectancy about what God has prepared for you next.

LORD,

Thank You for Your commitment not just to change,

but to revolutionize my life. Every fiber within my

soul inherently knows that I need to expand and

develop to become more like You. Teach me how

to cooperate with Your gracious work in me. Show me

where I am being resistant to the adjustments

You want to make. Now, I am excited to embark on

the path You have set before me.

UPON REFLECTION

In what areas of life or work do you resist change, or struggle to adapt to it?

When can change become destructive physically, mentally, emotionally or spiritually?

What changes do you fear most in the days or years ahead? Will you release them to God today?

*The Bible tells us to love our neighbors and also
to love our enemies; probably because generally
they are the same people.*

G.K. CHESTERTON

WHAT LOVE HAS TO DO WITH BUSINESS

ACCORDING TO A study at Penn State, the violence and aggression in computer games has been a concern of social commentators and an interest of media researchers for decades. Because the role of the opponent has been largely overlooked, they examined the difference in competitive frustration and aggression after users encountered the computer as opponent and a real person as opponent. They found that users experienced higher levels of aggressive feelings after playing the computer than after playing a stranger face-to-face. It appears that aggression in computer gaming may be reduced through the humanization of computer opponents. [26]

That study is about a game, but sometimes we unconsciously dehumanize our rivals as if they were machines rather than men and women caught up in the same struggles we are. Competition affects us personally as well as professionally. Before we go toe-to-toe with a company, we must remind ourselves that even large corporations are made up of individual people. While considering the personal element in the world of marketplace competition, there is a very important biblical standard to apply—the principle of love (you read that correctly). The very nature of competition means that sometimes you win and sometimes you lose. The one who gets the client, the order, the business, the grant, etc. wins, advances, survives or gets paid!

In *Business for the Glory of God*, Wayne Grudem wrote, "Competition seems to be the system God intended when he gave people greater talents in one area and gave other people greater talents in another area, and then he established a world where justice and fairness would require giving greater reward for better work."[27] So how do you know when you have crossed the line from healthy competition—superior performance, significant improvement, or sense of mission to destructive competition—callous, calculating and heartless? Any time you violate God's most fundamental directive, you have broken the law of love: *"Love does no wrong to a neighbor; therefore love is the fulfilling of the law."* (Romans 13:10) If you're wondering how to define "neighbor," it includes anyone you are tempted to dehumanize or hate. (see Luke 10:25-37) Make a list of all the biblical evidence and you'll be convicted:

> *"'Do not seek revenge or bear a grudge against one of your people, but love your neighbor as yourself. I am the LORD.'"* (Leviticus 19:18, NIV)
> *"For if you love those who love you, what reward do you have? Do not even the tax collectors do the same?"* (Matthew 5:46)
> *"Dear friends, since God loved us that much, we surely ought to love each other. "* (1 John 4:11, NLT)
> *"Owe no one anything, except to love each other, for the one who loves another has fulfilled the law."* (Romans 13:8)

Several years ago, during a breakfast event at a national shopping center convention, I interviewed the real estate managers from Target and Walmart about their work and their faith. As you can imagine, Target and Walmart have been long-time industry leaders and fierce competitors. Before that morning, the men had never met, yet it became clear to all that although these professionals were contending in the marketplace, they shared a bond that went far deeper than business. Their relationship was centered on mutual love for Christ, not corporate success or market share. The radical principle of love has the power to penetrate and transform even the marketplace. Isn't this radical dynamic exactly what Jesus predicted? *"By this all people will know that you are my disciples, if you have love for one another."* (John 13:35)

LORD,

Grant me the strength to work with energy and compete with wisdom and love for my colleagues and competitors. I want to be everything You designed, especially in my difficult business environment. Today, I seek to love You foremost, but ask You to supply the capacity to surprise my fiercest rivals with the compassionate kindness You have shown me.

UPON REFLECTION

What competitor has a way of bringing out the worst in you? Explain why.

How do you reconcile both winning and losing in your business or profession?

What step will you take to protect your heart from dehumanizing others and violating love when you compete?

*You believe because you have seen me. Blessed are
those who haven't seen me and believe anyway.*

JESUS, OF NAZARETH

AVOIDING THE ROAD OF SELF-RELIANCE

ARE YOU PREOCCUPIED with maintaining your competitive edge? Are
you constantly looking over your shoulder, wondering if you can stay in
the game? While competition provides many benefits to our economy and
society, it also generates angst in those who get too caught up in it. Doubts
and distrust easily arise: How can we outdo their image in this market? We
aren't big enough to match their economies of scale. They have unlimited
capital, and we're in debt. Their reputation is well-established and we have
no track record. We have to knock them out before they come after us!
Before we know it, we become slaves to apprehension, even aggression.
Our joy in work is robbed by the underlying dread of what our competitors
might do to us.

Faith in God's sovereignty [rule, supremacy, authority] is one of the most
important principles about competition. It's a marketplace reality that nothing is iron-clad guaranteed. Companies on top can fall off of their pedestal;
it happens every day. You face an undeniable fork in the road—one points
toward a path of self-reliance where pride, anxiety and distrust become
your companions . . . and they do not help anything. Jesus described the
other path: *"And which of you by worrying can add a single hour to his life's span?"* (Luke
12:25, NAS) My translation? Losing sleep over things you have no control
over just drains your creative energy.

I am reminded of Saul who seemed to have everything going his way,
at least at first. He became the first king of Israel, a nation established by
God. Later, his army won a great victory over the Philistines because of a

young, unassuming hero named David. Amid the celebration, Saul heard some women praising David above him and complained, *"'. . . Now what more can he have but the kingdom?' Saul looked at David with suspicion from that day on."* (1 Samuel 18:8-9, NAS) Rather than moving forward in faith that God had great plans for both of them, Saul began looking over his shoulder with growing paranoia and hatred. If only he would have taken the road of trust, knowing that God made him king in the first place. Instead, Saul became mentally and emotionally unstable and ultimately lost the kingdom and his life, because he focused on his competition rather than his Lord.

The second path requires dependence upon a wise and good God, Who promises *"I will instruct you and teach you in the way you should go; I will counsel you with My eye upon you."* (Psalm 32:8) On this road your companion is Jesus Himself, urging you and other disciples to continue following Him. If you will keep pace with Him today, rather than jumping ahead, He will provide all the wisdom and strength that you need to stay tuned into but not obsessed by your competition. Let Him worry about every "what if" scenario. Your job is to ask God to continue directing your business path. You won't be sorry.

LORD,

I confess that I watch and worry over my competition

way too much. It certainly hasn't added anything

positive to my life or my business. I really do believe

in Your promises, but I need help with my unbelief.

Expose the areas where I am walking in fear rather

than faith. Don't let me claim the faith of David

while living the false faith of Saul. I commit

to staying on the road of faith where You

are traveling by my side.

UPON REFLECTION

Describe an experience where you became obsessed with business dynamics you had no control over.
How did your apprehension affect your productivity or the outcome?
How did it affect your soul?

What dynamics or situations quickly move you toward fear rather than faith?
What can you do to stay on the right path?

Which area of your business do you need to release to God's providence today?
What would He say to you about it?

REFLECTING ON
MY JOURNEY

Looking back now I realize that my twenties focused mostly on making a name for myself, not on building a blameless reputation.
Not that I was willing to compromise my values; I just wanted to "be some-body" in the business world. In 1985, my firm was selected as a finalist for a major development for the city of Charlotte, North Carolina. They were planning a coliseum for their new NBA franchise and were selecting a real estate developer for offices and hotels around the coliseum. My partner and I were excited to be part of the final interviews with the mayor and city officials. We were competing with the "big boys." Our strategy was simple: convince the city officials that our smaller size made us agile and far more creative than the larger corporate developers. The stakes of the deal tempted me to flex my ego and promote myself. At the same time, I had a strong distaste for the arrogance that comes with self-promotion. In the end, we didn't get the project, but we left with gold—how to dis-cern the thin line between honesty and exaggeration, humility and pride, passion and greed; learning that one can do the right thing and still be misunderstood or do the wrong thing and be rewarded.

Lessons cannot be counted "learned" until they are tested. Some time before. my partner had invited me to merge my company with his. A little older and more established, he shared my Christian faith and valued my youthful exuberance. We immediately gained momentum and worked on many prosperous deals. After a while a local bank officer approached us, insistently offering us significant personal lines of credit. Later, he apolo-getically retracted his offer, explaining that the president had reviewed my financial statement and compared it with one I had submitted a few years before. She could not believe my assets had grown so quickly and suggested I had fabricated my financial information. Bottomline—she challenged my integrity and would not listen to the truth. That blow fell hard, solidifying for me the importance of maintaining character that is above reproach.

When the financial dominoes fell in the late eighties, threatening our company with extinction, we attempted to negotiate a workout with a strategic bank. We worked out an agreement with the bank officers but their examiners rejected the deal, one that might have saved our company. In that dark season, a startling thing happened. The bank's vice-president offered us a two-year contract to manage the very assets the bank had just taken control of. Explaining their rationale for this unexpected decision, the vice-president said they believed we were men of character. This meant everything to me, symbolizing what my mom had taught so carefully about placing my future in God's hands. In the end, we lost our wealth and our homes, but by the grace of God, we did not lose the good name we had built over the years.

PURSUING
FAITH
IN THE
MARKETPLACE

EXAMINING YOUR HEART

MAKING YOUR MOVE

LAUNCHING YOUR MISSION

DURING HIS LIFETIME, Alexander the Great conquered more land than anyone who had ever lived before, and amassed more wealth than he would ever be able to spend. When he was near death Alexander gave specific orders for his burial. Though the custom was to cover the hands, he wanted his hands to be empty and protrude outside the casket. The reason for this unusual request was to demonstrate that he was departing this world with nothing in his hands, in spite of all he had accumulated.[28] Alexander understood that material possessions, earthly accomplishments and power mean nothing when you are gone. Intellectually, you may accept this truth yet fail to let it direct the way you invest your time, energy, resources and relationships. Inspired to excellence, and devoted to integrity, you can carve out an admirable, honorable career, but is that enough for this life or the next? God offers you a staggering invitation to faith: *"Call to me and I will answer you, and will tell you great and hidden things that you have not known."* (Jeremiah 33:3)

Providence has at all times been my only
dependence, for all other resources seemed
to have failed us.

GEORGE WASHINGTON

BANKING ON THE NUMBERS

THE MARKETPLACE IS built on the practice of counting. We count our assets, our inventory, our bank accounts, our properties, our stores, our warehouses, our employees, our resources and even our contacts. The more we have, the more successful we are, right? The more we have, the more secure we feel, don't we? There is certainly nothing wrong with counting in order to faithfully manage our resources and responsibilities. The problem is what often happens to our hearts and minds as we count. I remember what it felt like to do some calculations of my own twenty-seven years ago. I was relatively young but my development company was growing and accumulating. We had great people, impressive properties and growing bank accounts. I remember how I felt when I checked my accounts. When the cash reserves were high, I was thankful to the Lord for providing so much for us, but I fear it was my false sense of security that put the extra bounce in my step. My confidence was growing . . . but confidence in what?

David is one of my favorite Bible characters, but not like the ones in great novels or movies. David was real. He was human. God said *"'I HAVE FOUND DAVID the son of Jesse, A MAN AFTER MY HEART, who will do all My will.'"* (Acts 13:22, NAS) God blessed David in a multitude of ways. You may picture his exploits on the battlefield against Goliath or remember how the nation of Israel prospered under his just leadership. In that culture, a king's greatest commodity was his army. One day, David determined to count his armies and instructed his commander to do it. Joab's response was respectful but perplexed, *"'Now may the LORD your God add to the people a hundred times as many as they are, while the eyes of my lord the king still see; but why does my lord the king delight in this thing?'"* (2 Samuel 24:3, NAS) He knew that God had forbidden this, but did as the king asked.

What is the big deal about counting your forces? God wanted it foremost in peoples' minds that He alone was the source of their strength. David was sensitive to God's heart (though a little slow): *"Now David's heart troubled him after he had numbered the people. So David said to the LORD, 'I have sinned greatly in what I have done. But now, O LORD, please take away the iniquity of Your servant, for I have acted very foolishly.'"* (24:10, NAS) David was given three consequences to choose from and though it distressed him, he said, *"'. . . Let us now fall into the hand of the LORD for His mercies are great, but do not let me fall into the hand of man.'"* (24:14, NAS) Indeed he was forgiven but the pestilence God sent resulted in the loss of 70,000 lives—how depressing to count that number!

The severity of the consequence shows the seriousness of the sin, not God's bad disposition. He wants us to place total confidence in Him, not our resources, not our abilities, not our position. After experiencing the loss of my business and my wealth, I was completely humbled and temporarily devastated. What happened to me stripped away more than money and property. It removed the false comfort I had placed in my resources and abilities. All through the years, God has faithfully provided for my family and moved me into work and ministry that have bought more fulfillment than I ever experienced in my affluence. Sometimes I catch myself reckoning what it would take to have "enough" . . . probably the amount that would keep me from having to exercise true dependence on God. How can you combat this inner battle today? Try counting something other than your material assets. Why don't you begin counting all the ways God has been faithful and then keep counting.

LORD,

You have exposed my heart through my own day-dreaming. As I imagine making or saving enough to be secure, I reveal that I value things that will perish more than things that will live on. Help me, Lord. Change my heart. Give me joy in working hard and giving my best, knowing that I will leave it all behind someday. Help me find my security in Your provision, and not in anything else.

UPON REFLECTION

What do you suppose led David to count his army after his long, successful record of victory?

When are you most prone to "counting"?
What does that reveal about your heart?

How much is enough?
Does that number imply that God is obligated to tilt the universe in your favor?

God opposes the proud,
but gives grace to the humble.

JAMES 4:6

THE ILLUSION OF CONTROL

BELIEVE IT OR NOT, Dr. Seuss's classic tale *Yertle the Turtle*, provides a very important lesson for the marketplace. Yertle ruled over a little pond of turtles. Unsatisfied with the stone that served as his throne, he decided his kingdom needed further expansion. Yertle decreed that all the turtles in the kingdom should stack themselves up to become his throne. First dozens, then hundreds came in obedience. Yertle thought his throne was secure, but at the bottom of the towering turtle stack was an obscure, feeble turtle named Mac. As the story goes: "That plain little Mac did a plain little thing. He burped! And his burp shook the throne of the king!" That little burp tossed Yertle down into the mud, abruptly ending his reign. Regardless of our position, level of respect, or financial clout we are all just one "burp" away from falling off our thrones![29]

Daniel 4 has a similar but true story about a human. Nebuchadnezzar, the powerful king of Babylon, was walking on the roof of his palace thinking: *"Is this not Babylon the great, which I myself have built as a royal residence by the might of my power and for the glory of my majesty?"* Although I'm pretty sure he knew the answer, God spoke to Neb from heaven: *". . . sovereignty has been removed from you, and you will be driven away from mankind, and your dwelling place will be with the beasts of the field. You will be given grass to eat like cattle, and seven periods of time will pass over you until you recognize that the Most High is ruler over the realm of mankind and bestows it on whomever He wishes."* (4:30-32, NAS) Sure enough, the word concerning Nebuchadnezzar came to pass and he was driven away from mankind and lived in the wild with the beasts. At the end of that period, we are told that the king raised his eyes toward heaven and his reason returned to him. *". . . I, Nebuchadnezzar, raised my eyes toward heaven and my reason returned to me, and I blessed the Most High and praised and honored Him who lives forever . . . for all His works are true and His ways just, and He is able to humble those who walk in pride.'"* (Daniel 4:30,37, NAS)

Like some of you, I am a recovering "control-aholic." Each of us fashions and protects our own illusions of jurisdiction. The business world has many names for this: *power play, enforcing your will, making it to the top.* The Bible just calls it *pride.* Like Yertle and Nebuchadnezzar, God may allow a burp in the economy or a sudden demotion to expose how little control you actually have and how helpless you are without God. Only God is ultimately in control and He is worthy to be followed. I find great relief knowing that the only person I can control is myself. I also find great serenity knowing that I am helpless but God is firmly seated on His throne and I should yield to Him.

LORD,

I confess my need to try to stay in control of circum-

stances and people. My ability to reign is just

an illusion. Only You know what next week and the

next century holds. Realizing this, I surrender;

I give up the fight. This frees me to cultivate

the dreams You have planted in my heart one day

at a time. Show me what is fitting for today.

Thank You for inviting me to share in Your work

in this world.

UPON REFLECTION

When were you fooled by the illusion of control?
What made you face reality?

How have even traces of pride affected your professional career?

In what areas of your home and work are you most tempted to try
to dominate?
How is that working for you?

*It is necessary for us to pass through many troubles
on our way into the kingdom of God.*

DR. LUKE, ACTS 14:22

WHO'S HOLDING WHO?

THOMAS EDISON WAS in a race with many other inventors to discover an efficient filament for the light bulb. The first successful test was on October 22, 1879 and the filament lasted forty hours. For several more months after he was granted the patent, Edison tried thousands of different substances—everything from horsehair to bamboo strips (which worked for 1,200 hours). When asked if he was discouraged by so many failed attempts, he responded, "If I find 10,000 ways something won't work, I haven't failed. I am not discouraged, because every wrong attempt discarded is another step forward."[30] That's what I call perseverance.

I am always astonished by stories of men and women who endured seemingly impossible situations. Abraham Lincoln's life appeared to hold one failure, loss or disappointment after another until he became President of the United States and led extraordinarily during the most trying era of American history. Susan B. Anthony was a determined women who, over the course of seventy-two years, gave speeches, published papers, was harassed and attacked by mobs and police and was jailed and beaten until the 19th Amendment was ratified, giving women the right to vote. The Bible is also filled with stories of individuals who overcame adversity, persecution, depression, disease and failure. Moses endured eighty years of ups and downs as he led the Israelites out of slavery to a Promised Land he never entered. Ruth's husband died and left her alone in a foreign land, yet she loyally cared for her mother-in-law and and became a critical link in Jesus' family tree. For years, Hannah prayed for a child, and when her prayer was finally answered, she dedicated her preschooler (Samuel the prophet) to a life of ministry. Peter denied knowing Jesus the night before His crucifixion, but ultimately became a renowned apostle who died a martyr rather than renounce Christ.

Perseverance is a mark of true faith because " . . *faith is the assurance of things hoped for, the conviction of things not seen. For by it the people of old received* [God's approval]" (Hebrews 11:1-2) Clichés like "keep the faith," "hang in there," or "IGBOK" (it's going to be ok) beg the question: Faith in what? Human courage and grit? The universe? Faith in whom? Myself? Statistics? Luck?

My pastor Scott Patty recounted a boyhood memory of the lake where his family went every summer. Its mystique was a little island that the older kids would swim out to, and one year he got tired of being left behind at the dock and told his dad that he was going with the big kids! He remembers diving out as far as he possibly could to get enough momentum to skim as far as possible. It only took a few minutes for Scott (and his dad) to realize that Scott's skinny little arms were not going to take him all the way to the island. In a flash, his father was beside him. Scott recalls thinking how tightly he was holding onto his dad's neck. Looking back, he realizes that it wasn't his grip, but his father's saving hold on him that brought him safely back to the shore.

Have you ever been drowning in a hopeless state of affairs? Don't foolishly believe that your own efforts will pull you through life's difficulties. Instead, follow Richard Smallwood's lyrics based on Psalm 40: "I love the Lord; he heard my cry and pitied every groan. Long as I live, when troubles rise, I'll hasten to his throne."[31] God's children are not exempt from the suffering and cares of our broken world or finite bodies, but God will help us carry on until we are safely home in His strong arms.

LORD,

You have faithfully kept me all these years, through good and terrible seasons. I am not here today by my own good works or strong character. I am here because You have sustained me and prolonged my life. Thank You for Your commitment to finishing the good work that You started in me. Surely You are the most forbearing One to keep withholding final judgment on all the evil in this world. Grant me the will to overcome based on the rock solid hope that You will see me through every ordeal and give me joy along the way.

UPON REFLECTION

Looking back over your life and career, what are the greatest obstacles you have had to overcome?

Why do you think it is easier to refer to "faith" than faith in God?

How has God held on to you even if you weren't holding on to Him?

He who has God and everything has no more
than he who has God alone.

C.S. LEWIS

MOTIVATED BY OUR FATHERS

IN *Pour Your Heart Into It*, Howard Shultz, founder and CEO of Starbucks, described growing up in the projects in Brooklyn, New York. His father's negative experience working in factories was a driving influence behind Shultz' decision to provide benefits and healthcare even for part-time Starbucks employees. Shultz always wondered how his father's life might have been different if someone had given him a break. When faced with monumental decisions, thinking about his father motivated Shultz to take care of his employees.[32]

How did your dad motivate the way you work? Some of your fathers caused you to become driven, (unconsciously hoping to gain his approval?). Some were encouraged by your father's support and pursue your dreams with little fear of failure. In one way or another, everyone is affected by the relationship they had (or didn't have) with their dad. Numerous self-help books and pop psychology shows address the impact of "the blessing" (i.e., "father-wound"). What may be less familiar is the importance of the relationship you have (or don't have) with the Heavenly Father.

How has "Father God" inspired your present life? Is your image of God in the likeness of your biological father? If you view God as a tyrant, waiting for you to step out of line, you may be averse to any risk. If you perceive God as disinterested in your wellbeing, you may become anxious over the smallest obstacle. If you believe God is impossible to please, you may be overly critical with your employees or clients. Martin Luther had a difficult time accepting the concept of grace [favor, blessing] because his father was a harsh disciplinarian who beat the children with a board he kept hanging nearby. The board was a constant reminder that he was ready to punish him at a moment's notice. Years later, after studying Romans, Luther decided to give his own children a more biblical idea of what God is like. Instead of a board, he placed an apple where everyone could see it. The apple reminded his children that their father was more eager to reward them for doing good than punishing them.[33] Which of these viewpoints motivates you more?

"Bless the LORD, O my soul, and all that is within me, bless his holy name! Bless the LORD, O my soul, and forget not all of his benefits, who forgives all your iniquity, who heals all your disesases, who redeems your life from the pit, who crowns you with steadfast love and mercy, who satisfies you with good so that your youth is renewed like the eagle's . . . He does not deal with us according to our sins, nor repay us according to our iniquities. For as high as the heavens are above the earth, so great is his steadfast love toward those who fear him; as far as the east is from the west, so far does he remove our transgressions from us. As a father shows compassion to his children, so the Lord shows compassion to those who [reverence] him . . . " (Psalm 103:1-5, 10-13) Maybe an inaccurate view of God tempts you to separate your business dealings from your inner feelings. Regardless of a poor or great relationship with your earthly dad, your heavenly Father is deeply interested in every detail of your life whether enormous or minuscule. Let His devoted love motivate everything you do today.

FATHER IN HEAVEN,

Thank You for being the ideal parent Whose fatherly instincts are fueled by constant love and compassion. You have given me your blessing, which makes me want to please You by everything I do and say. I am overflowing with the thought of Your concern for me. Let that same concern overflow to everyone I cross paths with today.

UPON REFLECTION

Describe how your relationship with your earthly father may be affecting you personally and professionally.

How has your image of God been shaped by your childhood? How do you picture God today?

Explain how your current view of God affects your approach to work.
If your concept of Him is unclear, where can you learn more about His true character?

Prayer does not fit us for the greater work,
prayer is the greater work.

OSWALD CHAMBERS

LESS TALK, MORE ACTION

SINCE THE ERA called the Enlightenment, each generation likes to think it is more progressive than the previous ones. Because human achievements continue, we suppose that no generation has ever risen so high. When calamity threatens, we believe that no other generation has ever had it so tough. We must become better students of history. In 1863, America experienced unbearable pain. Bitter opposition and sharp divisions characterized the country. People were angry, fearful and experiencing deep loss. Abraham Lincoln penned these commanding words during that season of adversity:

"We have been the recipients of the choicest bounties of Heaven . . . We have grown in numbers, wealth and power as no other nation has ever grown. But we have forgotten God. We have forgotten the gracious hand which preserved us in peace, and multiplied and enriched and strengthened us; and we have vainly imagined, in the deceitfulness of our hearts, that all these blessings were produced by some superior wisdom and virtue of our own. Intoxicated with unbroken success, we have become too self-sufficient to feel the necessity of redeeming and preserving grace, too proud to pray to the God that made us."[34]

His timeless words are still applicable for a generation driven by naturalism [all phenomena are explained by laws of science] and existentialism [we live in a meaningless and absurd world]. A short time ago, the majority of business people were intoxicated by a seemingly endless supply of prosperity. Today we are cold stone sober as foreclosure and bankruptcy files continue to pile up at the intersection of Wall Street and Main. Like me, you may have heard the confessions of many who have recognized their deeper need for God. You may be one who thought you were depending on Him, said you were trusting Him, but not doing the primary thing that demonstrates that desire—calling on Him. Here are just a few examples:

> "But know that the LORD has set apart the godly for himself;
>   the LORD hears when I call to him." (Psalm 4:3)
> "I call upon the LORD, who is worthy to be praised, and I am saved
>   from my enemies." (Psalm 18:3)
> "For he delivers the needy when he calls, the poor and him who
>   has no helper." (Psalm 72:12)
> "For you, O Lord, are good and forgiving, abounding in steadfast love
>   to all who call upon you." (Psalm 86:5)
> "Because he inclined his ear to me, therefore I will call on him
>   as long as I live." (Psalm 116:2)
> "Out of my distress I called on the LORD; the LORD answered me
>   and set me free." (Psalm 118:5)

A spirit of pride runs throughout the marketplace—no, it infects every arena of life. When you finally recognize it, and are willing to turn away from it, you are ready to cross the threshold through the open door and into the refuge of our wise, trustworthy, sheltering, guiding and welcoming Father. Will you spend some moments talking with Him right now?

LORD,

I can't go another minute without praying. I have been

drunk with my own accomplishments, and I'm just now

waking up to look at myself honestly. I see that pride

in my own brainpower has kept me from coming to You

for help, but now I see that my answers are nothing.

When I neglect our time together, the Enemy gains ground.

So, I humble myself and seek Your forgiveness, knowing

You've already given it. Thanks for such grace when I call

to You. Keep me now in the palm of Your hand.

UPON REFLECTION

Why do we experience memory loss about the dangers of self-sufficiency when times are good, forgetting our need for God until times are difficult?

What is your greatest hindrance to a regular habit of prayer?

If you could ask God for anything today, what would it be?

One today is worth two tomorrows.

BENJAMIN FRANKLIN

TAKING THE INITIATIVE

WHAT DID YOU intend to do yesterday, but didn't? When someone talks about what they are going to do tomorrow, there is a high likelihood that they uttered those same words yesterday. Procrastination keeps most of us from accomplishing all we are capable of. What are you postponing today—writing a letter, filling out a report, making a particular phone call? Is it something larger, like making an investment, starting a new company, pursuing more education or confronting a colleague? The first step is always the hardest. The Chinese philosopher Laozi said "The journey of a thousand miles begins with one step."

I remember getting started in the marketplace and listening to friends and associates talk about their business ideas and dreams of new ventures. I remember thinking that some of those folks were smarter than I would ever be. But I also noticed over time that many of those individuals were still just talking, brainstorming and visualizing, but never following through on those dreams. Daniel 11:32 (NAS) says, *"The people who know their God will display strength and take action . . ."* He was a great example of long-term, super-fruitful service to God and country. From his youth, Daniel's initiative set him apart.

You might wonder how knowing God is connected with action. God designed your personality and passions, packaged them into your body, then placed you in a particular time and set of circumstances. The Creator has an intended purpose for every person: to believe in Him, then to know and enjoy Him forever. Jesus said, *"This is the work of God, that you believe in him whom he has sent."* (John 6:29) Later Paul confirmed that *"God is faithful, by whom you were called into the fellowship of his Son, Jesus Christ our Lord."* (1 Corinthians 1:9)

There are many things we cannot understand about God's calling, yet we should never neglect acting on the guidance God has already provided. Once you develop a personal bond with Jesus Christ, you will begin to gain confidence in the way He is leading you to proceed. Besides that, confidence in God produces energy to take action.

Act today on what you know because tomorrow is never promised. James wrote an intense warning about this: *"Now listen, you who say, 'Today or tomorrow we will go to this or that city, spend a year there, carry on business and make money.' Why, you do not even know what will happen tomorrow. What is your life? You are a mist that appears for a little while and then vanishes. Instead, you ought to say, 'If it is the Lord's will, we will live and do this or that.' As it is, you boast in your arrogant schemes. All such boasting is evil. If anyone, then, knows the good they ought to do and doesn't do it, it is sin for them."* (James 4:13-17, NIV) We live in the Information Age, with a new occupation—knowledge workers. This change may accentuate the gap between knowledge and action, calculation, and following through. Don't let anything hold you back from completing your priority list. Take the first step now.

LORD,

Cure me from procrastination! Keep me from dragging my feet on work You have already assigned me to do. Cultivate my initiative by confirming each step. Tune my ear to hear Your voice behind me. When I get to the end of my life, I don't want to look back with regrets about things You put in my mind to do, but I never attempted. Give me the will to carry out Your will now.

UPON REFLECTION

How has laziness or making excuses held you back from reaching your potential in the workplace?

What fuels your initiative and spurs on ingenuity?

In what areas of professional life do you need to display more resourcefulness?
How have you prioritized the steps you need to take next?

You can live on bland food so as to avoid an ulcer, drink no tea, coffee or other stimulants in the name of health, go to bed early, stay away from night life, avoid all controversial subjects so as never to give offense, mind your own business, avoid involvement in other people's problems, spend money only on necessities and save all you can. You can still break your neck in the bathtub, and it will serve you right.

EILEEN GUDER

IT'S TIME TO MAKE A MOVE

SEVERAL YEARS AGO, I heard an interview with Jack Welch, the former Chairman and CEO of General Electric. One particular statement caught my attention: "When you are in the middle of a downturn, don't hunker down—make a move."[35] He was speaking about the propensity to play it safe and try to cling to what we have. When opportunity arises in one area, adversity often strikes in another. Have you experienced that before?

If the future of your industry is uncertain, should you go through with the acquisition? If sales are slumping, do you invest in new technology and risk cutting into your bottom line even more? What if you just lost some of your best employees; should you continue with your expansion plans? You have an idea that could help your company, but presenting it to senior management would be dicey. One thing is certain: operating in the marketplace is always full of risk! Welch warned business leaders in my industry of the danger of playing it too safe. The *paralysis of analysis* is a common struggle for many. Are you naturally a risk taker? Here are some basic insights drawn from Scripture to help you evaluate your work.

1. **Be diligent to calculate the cost and assess the risk before you take action.** Luke 14:28-30 (NLT) warns, "*But don't begin until you count the cost. For who would begin construction of a building without first alculating the cost to see if there is enough money to finish it? Otherwise, you might complete only the foundation before running out of money, and then everyone would laugh at you. They would say, 'There's the person who started that building and couldn't afford to finish it.'*" We must sit down soberly, and carefully evaluate potential benefits, sacrifices and obstacles. This requires more than a cursory look at the figures or a review of a brief pro forma. In other words, be a **calculated** risk taker, not a careless one. Remember the difference between faith and presumption. Well-meaning people misconstrue that exercising faith means acting on impulse. In reality, they may be presuming on God to attach His blessing to unwise plans.

2. **Never taking a chance is neither an option nor a mark of faith.** Ecclesiastes 11:4-6 (NLT) says "*Farmers who wait for perfect weather never plant. If they watch every cloud, they never harvest. Just as you cannot understand the path of the wind or the mystery of a tiny baby growing in its mother's womb, so you cannot understand the activity of God, who does all things. Plant your seed in the morning and keep busy all afternoon, for you don't know if profit will come from one activity or another—or maybe both.*" If you think about it too hard, getting out of bed in the morning can be a risk. Choosing to love someone takes courage. Living abundantly includes the possibility of jeopardy! As you are confronted with new opportunities, God will help you make wise but bold decisions. When you partner with the Lord, you are on the right track. With that in mind, what's your next move?

LORD,

Thank You for making me a dreamer and giving me an entrepreneur's spirit. Now I need the wisdom and diligence to make careful analyses and plans. Keep me from presuming on Your goodness and mercy and do not give me peace if I am moving ahead without Your blessing. Please give me an extra measure of confidence in You so that even if my plans don't succeed in the eyes of men, I'll know that You are pleased with my efforts.

UPON REFLECTION

Which is outside your comfort zone—counting the cost or taking action?
Can you guess why?

What is your greatest fear about taking a risk?
What's the worst that could happen if you stepped out today?

How will you strike a healthy balance between the "paralysis of (over)analysis" and hasty risk-taking?

I went to the woods because
I wished to live deliberately...
and not, when I came to die,
discover that I had not lived.

HENRY DAVID THOREAU

THE MOMENT OF TRUTH

WE HAVE COME a long way in maximizing research and analysis to forecast business results. The sophistication of tools that calculate every conceivable variation is remarkable. If you are getting ready to start a new business, make a financial investment, implement a new marketing strategy or convert to a new software package, you have access to more than enough information to make a good decision. Sometimes, there is so much information that we become overwhelmed. *The Information* by James Gleick states that "as the role of information grows beyond anyone's reckoning it grows to be too much. 'TMI', people now say. We have information fatigue, anxiety and glut."[36]

No matter how comprehensive your analysis, you eventually have to make a decision. Decisions involve a moment of truth. The defining moment, when you step out of your comfort zone into unknown territory, can be scary. Perhaps there is no better biblical example than Peter's experience of walking on water (Matthew 14:22-31). Peter was a professional fisherman, so life on the water was in his comfort zone. Battling rough seas was common for many of the disciples, but Jesus decided to shake things up a bit. When the disciples saw someone approaching on top of the waves, they thought it must be a ghost. *"But immediately Jesus spoke to them saying, '. . . Take heart; it is I. Do not be afraid.'"* (14:27) Peter made a daring suggestion. *"'Lord, if it is you, command me to come to you on the water.' He said, 'Come.' So Peter got out of the boat and walked on the water and came to Jesus."* (14:28-29)

Don't let the "impossible" cause you to write off this account. If Jesus created sea creatures, He can maneuver in their environment. Sometimes you are called to do novel, frightening things that feel like Peter's call to walk on water. For you, it may be a risk you have never taken before: forming a non-profit, accepting a lower paying job that could help your community, or petitioning a public figure about a deep conviction.

Seek God's will then keep your eyes on Him. Peter didn't impulsively leap in the water. He qualified, "If it is you, command me to come to you . . ." He recognized that only Jesus could make this happen. Once he was sure that Jesus called him, Peter did not hesitate and got out of the boat. At every moment of truth, we cross a line and there's no turning back. More often, we get ahead of God and pursue our own plans, never looking back until things get stormy. The marketplace may call that guts but the Bible calls it foolishness. What adventure is on your horizon? Have you been seeking God's desires through everyday obedience? He may be waiting to call you to the extraordinary until you are faithful in the ordinary. Do you dare to pray for a grand call to step out for God in new ways? Then begin to live more deliberately and faithfully in this moment of truth.

LORD,

Do not let me hide behind the wall of my own

intelligence and expertise, if it means disobeying Your

plans for me. Give me the faith to take wise risks

that You prompt me to take. Give me the eyes to see

the work in front of me as part of my faith journey.

Renew Your spirit of adventure in my heart.

Show me what walking on water with You means

in my life.

UPON REFLECTION

What types of risk are most difficult for you to take (financial, leadership, relational, other)?

If you had been with Peter, would you have tried to keep him in the boat, secretly wishing for the courage he had, or gotten in line to take your turn?

Describe a particular moment of truth you encountered recently. Did you make the most of it or wish for a "do over"?

It's not the critic who counts; not the man who points out how the strong
man stumbles, or where the doer of deeds could have done better.
The credit belongs to the man who is actually in the arena . . . who,
at best, knows in the end the triumph of great achievement, and who,
at worst, if he fails while daring greatly. So that his place will never
be with those cold timid souls who know neither victory nor defeat.

THEODORE ROOSEVELT

THE RISK IN RISK-TAKING

THERE IS A glamorous side to risk taking, the thrill of taking a chance, the excitement of making a move. But there is also a downside. Things might not work out the way they are "supposed to." The projections could be off, the idea might be rejected, or the group may question your ability. The bottom line is *you might fail*. When I was preparing to graduate from college and became interested in real estate, I spent a memorable day riding around with my roommate's father. Bob Easley has been a very successful real estate investor-developer, and back then he graciously took me along to check on his many properties. I did my best imitation of a sponge, trying to soak up the wisdom, experience, and knowledge that naturally oozed out of Mr. Easley. All the while, he told me war stories about some former deals he had been involved in. A great deal of risk-taking was required for all Bob has accomplished. Among his many pearls of wisdom, the one that stuck with me was: "You have to ask yourself, 'What is the worst thing that could happen?' If you can live with that answer, you are ready to get serious about considering the risk."

Some people lean toward an overconfident approach to risk, figuring everything will somehow work out. (The novice needs to take some extra steps before proceeding.) Others lean toward a cynical approach, figuring something will always go wrong. (The pessimist should accept the reality that attempting something is better than doing nothing.) We already noted that Peter did what no one but God had ever attempted—he walked on water. However, what began as a triumphant adventure quickly turned south. *"But when [Peter] saw the wind, he was afraid, and beginning to sink he cried out, 'Lord, save me.' Jesus immediately reached out his hand and took hold of him saying to him, 'O you of little faith, why did you doubt?'"* (Matthew 14:30) Peter's greatest show on earth almost became a search and rescue mission. After a moment of success, Peter focused on the **wind** and that is when he began to sink. He took his eyes off of Jesus and focused on the atmosphere around them. When you step out to do something new and challenging, that is the time to stay in touch with the Master.

A marketplace reality is that some of your risks—even risks that God leads you to take—may end in disappointment or failure. That does not mean God's will was not accomplished. Even though Peter began to sink, he learned that he was not alone. Jesus was there "immediately" to hold him up. Peter, the expert fisherman, was not meant to venture out alone; neither are we, despite all of our knowledge and training in business. There is great strength in knowing that God will never desert you even if the risk you take ends badly. Neither failure or success determines if you are within God's will. I know from experience that God's plans are far superior than mine, and often the opposite of what I expected.

As far as we know, Peter never walked on water again, but he survived and *learned*. Jesus redeemed every experience causing great maturity of character—steps independent souls may resist. Both success and failure prepared Peter to establish the early church a few years later. Keep listening for Jesus' call. Step out onto the water and keep your eyes locked on Him. Like Peter, your story is just beginning to unfold.

LORD,

Help me to find the balance between being too impulsive or overly cautious to the point that I don't exercise any faith. I am confronted with both foolish and exciting risks every day. I want to be a God-led risk taker, even though I know that I may not always succeed according to the world's economy. Most of all, use the experiences in my life to build me into a person of faith You can use to build the faith of others.

UPON REFLECTION

What is the biggest risk you have ever taken?
Did you fail or succeed (and by what standards)?

Which has the greatest impact on you, the fear of failure or the fear of missing an adventure?

Describe a failure you experienced that significantly improved your life or career.

*Imagine watching all that God might have done
with your life if you had let Him.*

JOHN ORTBERG

WORTH THE RISK

YOU MAY BE wondering why we are still reflecting on risk taking. I believe this is a crucial issue that we must linger over a little longer because faith is closely connected to your willingness to pursue God-directed possibilities (or uncertainties, depending on your viewpoint). Individual success in the marketplace requires taking some chances when the results cannot be guaranteed. Marty Rash, the founder and former CEO of Province Health Care, understood the challenge of developing this way of thinking in his organization. Over the course of nine years, he led Province from a startup company to a one billion plus dollar enterprise. In the process, he instituted a leadership approach he called "fail forward faster." All three words are significant.

Fail. Recognizing that most people are resistant to change, Marty discovered that the underlying reason is a fear of failure. Everyone knows that people make mistakes, yet businesses can breed a culture where people are afraid to offer their best because they cannot afford to make an error. This leads to an unhealthy culture of holding back, hiding mistakes or projecting blame on others.

Fail forward. Marty's approach cultivated an atmosphere where employees were trained to expect and embrace occasional failure. By doing so they had the freedom to act boldly, identify missteps, address problems, and make corrections that actually propelled the company forward toward success.

Fail forward faster. Because Marty allowed some leeway for failure without shame or discharge, leaders exercised more creative freedom, aiming for excellence and aggressively seeking solutions whenever they were needed. I know several employees who were part of Province Health Care, and to a person, they were stimulated by the culture and loved working for Marty.

Faith is not quite the same as self-confidence or human strength, but faith in a loving, living God builds self-confidence and strength. Hebrews 11:6 explains why pleasing God requires faith: *"And without faith* [confidence, trust, reliance, assurance, conviction] *it is impossible to please Him, for whoever would draw near to God must believe that he exists and that he rewards those who seek Him."* What do you believe about God, besides the fact of his existence? How do you think He rewards those who want to draw closer to him?

What kind of atmosphere do you work in or oversee? Is there freedom to take risks or to fail? If you are in a position to influence change, ask God to show you how to model "fail forward fast" in your setting. If you are not in a position of authority, you still have three options. First, you can **complain** but the disease of cynicism will destroy your spirit. Second, you can **leave** or start your own company—as long as you realize that your attitude will follow wherever you go. That is why I recommend a third option, to **trust** God in your current circumstances and focus on leading the one person you can influence (yourself) to adopt Marty Rash's mindset. Regardless of your workplace, you can turn your God-ordained journey into an adventure, your work into a mission, and your confidence in God into faith that is well worth the risk.

LORD,

Thank You for helping me grasp the connection
between risk-taking in my work and faith-stretching
with You. Help me to quit striving only for
the "slam dunks" where no risk is involved.
More than anything, help me to fail forward faster
toward You. Thank You for the influence of great
leaders like Marty Rash.

UPON REFLECTION

Does your work environment encourage or discourage risk taking?
Failure? Explain.

How have you "failed forward faster" in another area of life
besides work?

What professional risk are you considering right now?
What personal risk might God be asking you to take?

There are two kinds of people: those who say
to God, "Thy will be done," and those to whom
God says, "All right, then, have it your way."

C.S. LEWIS

THE PRIVILEGE OF REPRESENTING CHRIST

WE ALL REPRESENT someone, whether we are brokering a real estate deal, helping a client invest their funds or handling the accounts payable for our company. At one time or another, most people dream of being in business for themselves; but if God created everyone to own their own company, there would be no workers to fill the essential positions. Nevertheless, the secret desire to call our own shots is a valid reason to inspect our hearts carefully today. *"Search me, O God, and know my heart; test me and know my anxious thoughts. Point out anything in me that offends you, and lead me along the path of everlasting life,"* sang David. (Psalm 139:23-24, NLT)

Why do so many of us have problems with authority? God may have called you to lead your own company or head up an organization, but I'm thinking of deeper issues—self-exaltation, self-importance, self-centeredness. All of us want to make our own choices about our own lives. Even the most outwardly compliant person has the inner predisposition to play "Lord of the Ring" or "Queen of the Universe." According to God, no one is immune. *"We're all like sheep who've wandered off and gotten lost. We've all done our own thing, gone our own way. And God has piled all our sins, everything we've done wrong, on him, on him."* (Isaiah 53:6, MSG)

Jesus Christ conquered Sin but its remains are still bound up in our bodies. Until we die, we must fight against the pull to self-govern. Paul outlined the problem and the solution for the Galatians: *"But I say, walk by the Spirit, and you will not gratify the desires of the flesh. For the desires of the flesh are against the*

165

Spirit, and the desires of the Spirit are against the flesh, for these are opposed to each other, to keep you from doing the things you want to do. But if you are led by the Spirit, you are not under the law." (Galatians 5:16-18) Within that warning is a breathtaking thought, that God's Spirit has taken up residence inside us to fight that ongoing battle. Why would I rebel against "*that glorious presence*"? (Isaiah 3:8) How does that profound truth relate to your work?

As a real estate consultant for retailers, I have sat in many meetings with shopping center developers feeling the weight of responsibility to represent my company well. On the flip side, I enjoy the privilege of representing something bigger than myself. A burden is also lifted when I accept that I must play my role well, but I am the ambassador, not the head of state! It occurs to me that my current job reflects what God intends for each of us—to view ourselves as His representative in the marketplace. You and I have the sacred duty and honor to act on His behalf, to embody our immense and powerful yet humble and caring Savior. "*All this is from God, who through Christ reconciled us to himself and gave us the ministry of reconciliation; that is, in Christ God was reconciling the world to himself, not counting their trespasses against them, and entrusting to us the message of reconciliation. Therefore, we are ambassadors for Christ, God making his appeal through us. We implore you on behalf of Christ, be reconciled to God.*" (2 Corinthians 5:18-20)

Ambassadors are representatives, agents, messengers or diplomats for a leader or nation. Ambassadors know their assignment and their identity. Their citizenship remains in their homeland, but they live in a foreign country. They adapt quickly and interact perceptively within their host culture. They represent the interests of their ruler. As Christians we bring a message of good news, of reconciliation. Christ our King has assigned you to represent Him wherever you work. In *Instruments in the Redeemer's Hands*, Paul David Tripp wrote, "His 'within you' kingdom is about the display of His glory and people who are holy."[37] Whether you supervise 500 employees, own a mom and pop business, or work for a multi-national corporation, you have been given a sacred calling as a representative to the "CEO of the Universe." Are you up for the challenge?

LORD,

Thank You for the high calling of serving as Your

representative in my industry and my community.

I need Your "eyes" to correctly view myself and my

role. Thank You for making my identity in Christ clear

throughout Scripture. I know that the balance between

independence and anarchy is a slippery slope, but today

I yield to You, my Benevolent Superior. Give me joy

and fulfillment as I serve Your best interests today.

UPON REFLECTION

What is it about your workplace that brings out your pride or rebellion against authority?

How are you affected by the idea that more than *your* integrity and competence is on the line when you do business?

As you embrace the reality that you are representing the "CEO of the Universe" in what ways is it a game changer for the way you work?

No matter what I say, what I believe,
and what I do, I am bankrupt without love.

1 CORINTHIANS 13:3 (NLT???)

UNDERSTANDING MARKETPLACE PRODIGALS

LOVE IS NOT the first word that comes to mind when you think of the marketplace. In fact, the thought of love feels quite out of place when it comes to this arena. In all my years of real estate I have never had a client exclaim, "I'm really feeling the love in this market!" Maybe we should step back and reflect on a quality that needs to be infused in our workplaces. *Love is the Killer App* introduced love language to the world of commerce. Tim Sanders stated, "I live to create value in people's lives and I measure myself by their reactions. I'm a love merchant. I trade in intangibles. I can trade that currency to infinity."[38] I really enjoyed his many helpful principles about networking; however, I must note our underlying mistake—love is **not** a commodity, a product used to get what we want. Love is a character trait, a virtue woven into the fabric of our new spiritual nature. With the Spirit's filling, it overflows in actions benefitting others

This is only possible when you consider the source. *"Beloved, let us love one another, for love is from God, and whoever loves has been born of God and knows God. Anyone who does not love does not know God, because God is love. In this the love of God was made manifest among us, that God sent his only Son into the world, so that we might live through him. In this is love, not that we have loved God but that he loved us and sent his Son to be the propitiation for our sins. Beloved, if God so loved us, we also ought to love one another. No one has ever seen God; if we love one another, God abides in us and his love is perfected in us."* (1 John 4:7-12)

That brings up one of the most compelling portraits of God's love—the Prodigal Son in Luke 15. A wealthy man's younger son demanded his share of the inheritance so he could leave home and live any way he wanted. The father divided all of the assets between his two sons. The older son remained and dutifully worked in the family business. The younger left home and squandered his share on wild living. As you can imagine, his money and friends ran out at about the same time. When he hit rock bottom, he remembered that even servants lived better than him, so he humbly returned home. He found his father running toward him with open arms, because his dad had been scanning the horizon, watching for his return. "I'm not going to wait until you've paid off your debt; I'm not going to wait until you've duly groveled. You are not going to earn your way back into the family. I am going to simply take you back. I will cover your nakedness, poverty, and rags with the robes of my office and honor."[39]

When I look at the marketplace, I see a large gathering of "younger brothers." I recognize them because I was once a prodigal. The danger is that a repentant prodigal can easily become the "elder brother" over time. In *The Prodigal God*, Tim Keller pointed out that those who have been outwardly obedient can be equally prodigal in their self-righteousness. Those who have experienced the lavish mercy and grace of our God have an incredible opportunity to serve in the role of loving fathers who earnestly seek younger brothers and sisters who have lost their bearings.[40]

The marketplace is starving for love without qualification, not based on competence or achievement. Imagine what could happen if you brought that kind of love into a workplace that only recognizes one currency—you receive only what you deserve. Here are a few practical ways you can do this: Look past the deal to the person, rather than past the person to the deal. Take time to stop and listen, and encourage an associate about a personal struggle they've shared. Serve people who can't do anything to further your career or help you gain business. Who knows, someday you may hear a co-worker say, "I'm really feeling the love in this place!" For God's sake, make it your business to turn back the tide today.

LORD,

Thank You for loving me enough to draw me back to Yourself. Your undeserved mercy has changed me forever. All around me there are people living thoughtlessly, recklessly, lonely and hopeless despite the facade that all is well. Fill me with Your Spirit this week, so that I can recognize who needs Your love extended to them with human arms.

UPON REFLECTION

How clued-in are you to the prodigals you brush shoulders with every day?

Who are you more like in the parable above: the father, the younger son or the elder brother?
What changes does your present attitude call for?

Where do you need to cultivate love in your workplace?
When will you begin to view fellow employees as God views you?

Christians should be true to God's Word,
even when it stings; and their living should create
a thirst for God in those who do not know Him.

JOHN MACARTHUR

THE BURNING SENSATION OF SALT

MY FRIEND WAS more than qualified for a vacant executive position with a national retailer. After four interviews, everything pointed toward an offer. However, to his surprise, he was informed that the company was choosing to go another direction. When he probed for the reason, the vice president confessed, *"We just feel like your faith is 'out there' and seems to be so integral to who you are that you wouldn't fit in well."* He went on to clarify that their employees like to have a good time, laugh at off-colored jokes, party, etc. Although my friend clearly possessed the skills to knock it out of the park, his lifestyle would have posed a crisis of conscience for those he would have worked with. If you still count on justice in the marketplace, this story may tempt you to punch a wall! Nevertheless, don't miss its valuable lessons.

Sometimes a godly lifestyle will provoke unbelieving friends and associates. Jesus once told His disciples, *"You are the salt of the earth; but if the salt has become tasteless, how can it be made salty again? It is no longer good for anything, except to be thrown out and trampled underfoot by men."* (Matthew 5:13, NAS) When Jesus called His followers *salt*, He referred to their influence on the world. Salt was considered an extremely valuable commodity because of its many unique qualities. Salt preserves, seasons, and heals. It also stings when applied to an open wound. The decision makers in the company that rejected my buddy believed that a follower of Christ would create a restrictive environment. By the way, my friend is a blast to be around, but an authentic disciple of Christ often has a restraining effect on the environment. Salt's preserving properties limit spoilage and slow down decomposition. While some may openly reject your faith, God will use your life to create a curiosity and restlessness for something more in others.

Salt creates thirst. The more sodium you take in, the more you seek to quench your thirst. Jesus approached an outsider for a drink of water. When the Samaritan woman asked Him why, Jesus said, *"If you knew the gift of God, and who it is that is saying to you, 'Give me a drink,' you would have asked him, and he would have given you living water."* He went on to explain that *"Everyone who drinks of this water will be thirsty again, but whoever drinks of the water that I will give him will never be thirsty again. The water that I will give will become in [you] a spring of water welling up to eternal life.' The woman said, 'Sir, give me this water, so that I will not be thirsty or have to come here to draw water.'"* (John 4:10, 13-14) That is my prayer for the marketplace at large—that our compassionate encounters with those who have not believed will generate a thirst to know more about the One who brings satisfaction and fullness.

Salt is rendered useless if contaminated by other minerals. You could become so concerned about fitting in at your workplace that you have no healing, preserving or flavoring effect on your colleagues. You have the potential to create a hunger and thirst for the unshakeable peace and abundant joy God longs to give the whole world. Is there anything distinctive about your life that others would recognize? Do you live in such a way that you could be turned away from a job because of your faith? If that ever happens, Jesus promises great rewards for those who are mistreated on his behalf (Matthew 5:10-12). The marketplace needs more, not less, saltiness. What do you taste like today?

LORD,

When I first learned what happened to my friend,

I was indignant, but the more I reflect on it,

I am rejoicing over the good work You are doing

through him and so many believers. I want to be

"tasty" salt wherever I go. Please use my life to create

a thirst in others. Grant me the fortitude to accept

that this may lead to ridicule or rejection.

Protect me from attitudes or words that are anything

but full of grace and peace.

UPON REFLECTION

What advice or comfort would you offer a friend who didn't get the job because of his or her faith?

Which quality of salt is most needed in your workplace and why (preserves, seasons, heals, burns, makes thirsty)?

If someone accused you of being "too Christian," what evidence would they be drawing on?

In Him was life and the life was the light of men.
The light shines in the darkness and the darkness
has not overcome it.

JOHN, THE APOSTLE

THE PENETRATING POWER OF LIGHT

IN THE COURSE of an extended conversation with an associate, we covered several subjects besides the business at hand. We talked about family, relationships, perspectives on money and ultimately our spiritual backgrounds. Then my friend asked some very direct questions about my faith. I shared how God has changed my life and explained how to experience the grace and forgiveness of God through Jesus Christ. Today my friend is also my brother in the faith and a faithful follower of Jesus Christ.

After Jesus told His followers that they were the salt of the earth, He added, *"You are the light of the world. A city set on a hill cannot be hidden. Nor do people light a lamp and put it under a basket, but on a stand, and it gives light to all in the house. In the same way, let your light shine before others so that they may see your good works and give glory to your Father who is in heaven."* (Matthew 5:14-16) Salt works subtly, but light works visibly. Salt has an indirect, provisional effect, while light has a direct, absolute influence. Salt is distributed by the way you live, work and relate to people. Light is emanated by the Holy Spirit residing in you and the words you communicate to others. The marketplace needs both salt and light.

Light has different effects on people depending on their location. Light is a welcome sight if you're lost in a dark maze or spending the winter in Alaska, but it is unwelcome to an insomniac or a burglar. In a spiritual sense, those who are struggling to keep sins hidden dread the thought of them being brought to light. If you have been a Christian for a long time, you may have forgotten how it feels to be overcome by darkness. You have come to enjoy the warmth of God's light. Don't dismiss that the majority of your clients, associates, neighbors, even family members, are still stumbling through life because of soul blindness. *"In their case the god of this world has blinded the minds of the unbelievers, to keep them from seeing the light of the gospel of the glory of Christ, who is the image of God. For what we proclaim is not ourselves, but Jesus Christ as Lord, with ourselves as your servants for Jesus sake. For God, who said, 'Let light shine out of darkness', has shown in our hearts to give the light of the knowledge of the glory of God in the face of Jesus Christ."* (2 Corinthians 4:4-6)

Those who have experienced the sacred gift of salvation should gladly share the Light that leads to God (see Philippians 2:15). In *The Pursuit of Excellence*, Ted Engstrom shared about cleaning out a desk drawer and finding a flashlight that had not been used in over a year. It didn't work so he opened it up to investigate. Although he had replaced the batteries and stored it in a warm, dry place, battery acid had corroded the inner workings. The flashlight was ruined from a lack of use.[41] Long before flashlights were invented, Jesus said "[My followers] are the light of the world." He didn't say, "Become light" or "Act like lights." The Spirit of Light is already inside every Christian. The only way to prevent your light from shining is to purposely cover it up. God has placed you right where you are so that He can draw others to Himself. Will you allow your light to shine today?

LORD,

I have been blessed with so much of Your Light, yet I often draw a very tight boundary around my world and fail to recognize how many people I pass by who are still captives of Darkness. Other times, I block the light out by indifference or fear. I don't want to corrode and become useless. I need Your compassion and courage to step out and share the greatest news human ears can hear. Empower me to represent Jesus well in my workplace today.

UPON REFLECTION

How aware are you of the spiritual darkness and light in your industry? Explain.

When it comes to sharing your faith at work, what is the line between what is fitting and what is unacceptable?

Are you more likely to err on the side of not speaking up when you see an opportunity or going overboard and making your office a pulpit? Explain.

The only thing necessary for the triumph of evil is for good men to do nothing.

EDMUND BURKE

IMAGINING WHAT'S NEXT

IN 1857, ONLY twenty years after the Financial Panic of 1837, Wall Street was on the verge of crashing. There was also a great deal of political unrest between the northern and southern states over state's rights and slavery. This, in turn, created upheaval within the church, especially evangelical* circles. During that period, Jeremiah Lanphier, a New York businessman, sat in a darkened room in the back of a church and prayed "Lord, what do you want me to do?" God's answer to his simple prayer was just as clear. "The people should pray." Lanphier was not an influential pastor or powerful corporate magnate, yet he proceeded to organize a midday businessmen's prayer meeting one block from Wall Street. He waited ten minutes after the first meeting was scheduled to begin. No one came. He waited twenty minutes. Still no one had arrived. Finally, thirty minutes after the starting time, one person came. By the end of the first meeting, six had turned up.

Lanphier's program wasn't eye-catching—read Scripture and pray. The second meeting, twenty people showed up. Before long, the meeting place overflowed. Weekly meetings turned into daily meetings. Within a few months there were twenty such prayer gatherings throughout the city. After six months, there were over 50,000 people gathering to pray daily! That movement of God spread to other large cities including Philadelphia and Chicago, and within one year there were reportedly one million people who came to faith in Christ. Considering that America's population was only thirty million at that time, God truly ignited a spiritual fire through an ordinary businessperson who faithfully lit the match.[42]

*churches that emphasize the teachings and authority of the Scriptures

It's not all about you; it is all about Him. I'm not implying that we are unimportant to God's plans; we have been made partners of the Almighty. Paul made this clear to the new Christians in Greece: *"For consider your calling, brothers: not many of you were wise according to worldly standards, not many were powerful, not many were of noble birth. But God chose what is foolish in the world to shame the wise; God chose what is weak in the world to shame the strong; God chose what is low and despised in the world, even things that are not, to bring to nothing things that are, so that no human being might boast in the presence of God . . . Let the one who boasts, boast in the Lord."* (1 Corinthians 1:26-31)

When you consider the state of our nation and the world today, the problems seem overwhelming. Changing anything feels like spitting on a desert. Are you wondering how you could possibly make a difference? Jesus is calling you to believe one more promise: *"The things that are impossible with people are possible with God."* (Luke 18:27) It's time for you to follow Jeremiah Lanphier and ask, "What do You want me to do?"

LORD,

When I read stories about how You have used regular
people over the course of history, I realize that this
generation is no less in need of Your power. Please
forgive my cynicism about Your ability to turn things
around in our country, my workplace, my home. I want
to be found faithful and obedient when my life is over.
I believe You can do the impossible, so I'm asking You
how I can reach out to others in my industry and beyond
to inspire the kind of faithfulness and obedience that
will bring glory to You.

AMEN.

UPON REFLECTION

What are your reactions to the story of Jeremiah Lanphier? Does it motivate or discourage you? Explain.

Why don't more Christian business people initiate "kingdom" endeavors today?

.

Have you ever kicked off something of spiritual purpose in the context of your workplace?
If so, how was it received? If not, what could you try?

REFLECTING ON
MY JOURNEY

In 1996, I attended a national shopping center convention.
Las Vegas has always represented the opulence and affluence to which so many aspire. That morning as I was reading my Bible and praying in my hotel room, I felt burdened for those in my industry and wished there was a way they could view business and life in a new way. As I reflected on the need, an idea captured my mind: Could I facilitate a gathering during our annual convention, a meeting where both believers and seekers could come and be welcome?

After a year of thinking, praying and planning, two encouraging friends helped me host a breakfast during the annual Shopping Center Convention. That first year, fifteen colleagues showed up. We were thrilled. Over the next three years, just by word of mouth, we drew together fifty, then seventy-five, then one hundred ten people. Fifteen years later, our annual breakfast gathers around five hundred—the majority of the men and women who attend are professing Christians, but the event has become increasingly evangelistic.

From the beginning our goal has been to offer something for everyone who attends our gathering. We charge no one for the delicious breakfast. Generous sponsors underwrite the event and donate books or Bibles for each guest. Table captains facilitate a roundtable discussion. A business leader speaks or we interview a panel of Christians from the industry. An hour later, the fellowship dismisses, but scores of people continue talking or praying with friends.

As the impact of our informal breakfast gathering grew, we formed a non-profit organization—the Retail Christian Network. Now our organization hosts national and regional events for over 1,500 members around the country.

Encouraging people from coast to coast has been challenging from Day One. To stay in touch, I started sending out e-mail messages inspired by my own devotional times and my experiences in the workplace. I didn't have a specific plan for how they could be used; I simply sensed God had called me to write that first *Reflection*, send it, then write and send the next one, month after month for seven years.

I was surprised by the testimonies from those who received these devotional emails. People shared how God used those reflections to renew their faith. The spiritual fruit in their lives showed. I witnessed their growing boldness to do business in an honorable way and to share their faith within our industry and beyond.

Today, over two thousand subscribers receive *Reflections on a Higher Call* each month: read it, forward it to friends, or discuss it in small groups. Their responses and requests for more prompted me to write this book as a way to serve our network.

Retail Christian Network (RCN) is much bigger than one person—bigger than me, bigger than the leadership team that supports this network of men and women. A growing movement has sparked spiritual renewal within one particular industry but our team believes this model can be applied to other occupations and industries. For example, last year I was honored to help a friend transfer the RCN model to his industry. The Financial Christian Network began with great potential for impact.

Think of the industries within the American marketplace as "unreached people groups," the terminology used by missionary organizations. Penetrating these groups will require people who understand the unique culture of their professions. These unreached people groups need people who speak their language of business and share their skills and goals.

I pray that God will continue to raise up other men and women to reach out to their own industries, their personal unreached people groups. Together, we can watch God transform the global marketplace for His glory.

A PROFESSIONAL'S PRAYER

HAVE YOU EVER wondered how birds are able to sleep without falling off of their perch? You see, when a bird bends its leg at the knees, the tendons cause the claws to contract and grip like a steel trap. The bird cannot let go until its legs are straightened again. A sleeping bird can teach a valuable lesson about prayer. The marketplace equates power with remaining "on top" in knowledge, wealth and status. God equates power with a willingness to "come under" like a bird, to bend the knee—deliberately yielding control and becoming dependent upon God.

King Solomon, the wealthiest, most influential man of his generation spread out his hands and prayed, "... O LORD, God of Israel, there is no God like you, in heaven above or on earth beneath, keeping covenant and showing steadfast love to your servants who walk before you with all their heart ... But will God indeed dwell on the earth? Behold, heaven and the highest heaven cannot contain you; how much less this house that I have built! Yet have regard to the prayer of your servant and to his plea, O LORD my God, listening to the cry and to the prayer that your servant prays before you this day ... And listen in heaven your dwelling place, and when you hear, forgive ..." (1 Kings 8:23-30)

Here is the prayer of a more contemporary disciple. After reading mine, you may want to compose one of your own.

HEAVENLY FATHER,

I receive this day as a gift from You. I welcome Your companionship as I begin my work today. Fill me with Your Spirit so I can know your perfect peace. Surround me with Your protection in my car, at the office, and during every meeting and call. You are my strong tower (a skyscraper!) and in You I find my identity and security (collateral). Your power is far above my best efforts. Please grant me strength to do every task to which I put my hands. Enable me to think clearly, choose wisely, work diligently and communicate effectively. I know that every talent and skill I possess comes from You. I am honored to be Your partner for the cause of Your glory. Thank You for entrusting me with a role in Your kingdom. When I encounter a challenge or setback today, guide me toward an honorable and effective solution. When I begin to wear down, infuse me with Your energy. When my emotions begin to fray, replenish my soul. When I am tempted to settle for mediocrity, remind me that I work for You. When I'm enticed to cheat or lie, prick my conscience. May every interaction with others bring them hope, help and encouragement. When my day finally ends, give me a sense of satisfaction and trust that you are in control of my job and my life, and that I offered You my best. I lift up these requests to You in the name of Jesus, my Savior and Friend . . .

AMEN.

FOOTNOTES

A HIGHER CALL
1 Gordon MacDonald, Ordering Your Private World (Oliver Nelson, a division of Thomas Nelson, Inc. Publishers, 1988) p. 9.

WHOSE CALLING IS IT?
2 Rick Warren, The Purpose Driven Life (Zondervan, 2002) p. 17.

CALLED TO SOMETHING GREATER
3 Student Discipleship Ministries, My Quiet Time-J, (SDM, 1996) p. 18.

BLUEPRINT FOR SUCCESS
4 Leadership Magazine, Summer 1996, Vol. XVI, No. 3, pp. 38-39.

A TIMELY TURNAROUND
5 Student Discipleship Ministries, My Quiet Time-I (SDM, 1991) p. 17, cc p. 8.
6 Jim Taylor and Watts Wacker, The 500 Year Delta: What Happens After What Comes Next (Harper Collins 1997).

DISCERNING THE ENDGAME
7 Charles W. and Janet E. Morris, Jesus in the Midst of Success (Broadman and Holman Publishers, 2000) p. 5.

GOD FINISHES WHAT HE STARTS
8 Richard Sandomir, "Bud Greenspan, 86, Dies, Filmed Olympics in Glory," New York Times, December 26, 2010. www.nytimes.com/2010/12/26/sports/olympics/26greenspan.html

GOD PRIORITIZES REST
9 Preachers Illustration Service, Vol. 8, No. 5 Sep/Oct. 1995 #1774, L. Craroman, "Spring in the Valley." Adapted SDM use My Quiet Time-J, p. 30.

PUTTING YOUR HANDS TO THE GOOD WORK
10 Bits & Pieces, July 24, 1992, pp. 19-20.

EXERCISING ANT-SIZED DISCIPLINE
11 Billy Beacham, Back to the Basics (Student Discipleship Ministries, 1988) p. 99.

DISTINCTION IN EVERY DETAIL
12 John C. Maxwell, The 21 Indispensable Qualities of a Leader (Thomas Nelson, Inc. Publishers, 1999) p. 18.
13 Makoto Fujimura, Crossway Press Conference, The Gospel Coalition, Chicago, April 2011.

CHARACTER TRUMPS LOGIC
14 Jacob M. Braude, Human Interest Stories, Complete Speaker's and Toastmaster's Library.

SELLING OUT
15 Mary Pipher, Writing to Change the World (Riverhead Books, 2006) p. 12.
16 Wayne Grudem, Business for the Glory of God (Crossway, 2003) p. 61.

RECOGNIZING THE REAL DEAL
17 Student Discipleship Ministries, My Quiet Time-G (SDM) p. 41.

WHAT ARE THEY SAYING ABOUT YOU?

18 "Dungy is Praised as he exits NFL," *The Fifth Down: The NY Times NFL Blog.* January 13, 2009 *www.fifthdown.blogs.nytimes.com/2009/01/13/dungy-is-praised-as-he-exits-nfl/*

THE OWNERSHIP OF RESPONSIBILITY

19 *Politico.* "Q & A with T. Boone Pickens" by Patrick Gaven, 6/19/11. Adapted. *www.politico.com/news/stories/0611/57296.html*

DEFENDING YOUR AIRSPACE

20 Gordon MacDonald, *Rebuildling Your Broken World* (Oliver Nelson, a division of Thomas Nelson, Inc. Publishers, 1988) p. 47.

LIVING ABOVE REPROACH

21 John Maxwell, *Talent is Never Enough* (Thomas Nelson Publishers, 2007) p. 197.
22 Ibid. pp. 202-203

REVOLUTIONARY PRINCIPLE OR ANCIENT TRUTH?

23 Jim Collins, *Good to Great* (HarperCollins Publishers, 2001) pp. 12-13.

CAUGHT UP IN THE HEAT OF COMPETITION

24 Pulpit Helps, February 1990, p. 14.

FACING THE DEMANDS OF CHANGE

25 Jeff Jernigan, *Discipleship Journal*, Issue 69, 1992, p. 47.

WHAT LOVE HAS TO DO WITH BUSINESS

26 Russell B. Williams and Caryl A. Clippinger, "Aggression, competition and computer games: computer and human opponents," *Computers in Human Behavior*, Volume: 18, Issue: 5, (2002) (Publisher: Elsevier) pp. 495-506.
27 Wayne Grudem, *Business for the Glory of God* (Crossway, 2003) p. 41

PURSUING FAITH IN THE MARKETPLACE

28 *Pulpit Helps*, Jan. 1991, "Divine Appointments" (SDM, 1994) p. 66.

THE ILLUSION OF CONTROL

29 Dr. Seuss. *Yertle the Turtle*—50th year Edition (Random House, 2008).

WHO'S HOLDING WHO?

30 Thomas Edison, *www.scribd.com/doc/75348821/Thomas-Edison*

31 From the album *Richard Smallwood With Vision—The Praise & Worship Songs of Richard Smallwood*, "I Love the Lord" Label: Verity Records. Copyright: ℗ 2003 Zomba Recording LLC, original release date January 1, 1990.

MOTIVATED BY OUR FATHERS

32 Howard Shultz and Dori Jones Yang, *Pour Your Heart into It* (Hyperion 1999).
33 *Turning Point. Divine Appointments*, (Student Discipleship Ministries, 1994) p. 23.

LESS TALK, MORE ACTION

34 President Abraham Lincoln, proclamation appointing a National Fast Day, March 30, 1863, *The Collected Works of Abraham Lincoln*, ed. Roy P. Basler, vol. 6, p. 156.

IT'S TIME TO MAKE A MOVE
35 Jack Welch with Brit Hume, Interview at 2005 ICSC Convention, Las Vegas Nevada. *www.icsc.org/srch/sct/sct0405/icsc_news_1.ph*

THE MOMENT OF TRUTH
36 James Gleick, *The Information: A History, a Theory, a Flood* (Pantheon Books, 2011) Prologue.

THE PRIVILEGE OF REPRESENTING CHRIST
37 Paul David Tripp, *Instruments in the Redeemer's Hands* (P & R Publishing, 2002) p. 5.

UNDERSTANDING MARKETPLACE PRODIGALS
38 Tim Sanders, *Love is the Killer App* (Crown Business, a division of Crown Publishing Company, 2002).
39 Tim Keller, *The Prodigal God* (Riverhead Trade, a division of Penguin Group, 2011) p. 23
40 Ibid, p. 24.

THE PENETRATING POWER OF LIGHT
41 *Turning Point, Divine Appointments* (Student Discipleship Ministries, 1994). Adapted from Ted Engstrom. Pursuit of Excellence. (The Zondervan Corporation, 1982) p. 26.

IMAGINING WHAT'S NEXT
42 Margaret Bendroth, "What Wilt Thou Have Me To Do?" *More Than Conquerors* (John D. Woodbridge, General Editor; Moody Bible Institute of Chicago, 1992) p. 336.

SCRIPTURE INDEX

* referenced, not quoted

FREE SUBSCRIPTION TO

REFLECTIONS
ON A

HIGHER
CALL

You can receive future *Reflections* in your inbox
by subscribing at highercallministries.org

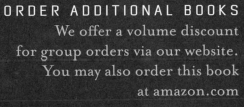

ORDER ADDITIONAL BOOKS

We offer a volume discount
for group orders via our website.
You may also order this book
at amazon.com

David is available to speak at professional events or business
gatherings; church retreats or conferences; leadership workshops
or forums. To read more about the "Higher Call Conference" go
to our website or contact the Higher Call office at 615.791.9782.